Preparing for Adoption

of related interest

Creating Loving Attachments
Parenting with PACE to Nurture Confidence
and Security in the Troubled Child
Kim S. Golding and Daniel A. Hughes
ISBN 978 1 84905 227 6
eISBN 978 0 85700 470 3

Attaching in Adoption
Practical Tools for Today's Parents
Deborah D. Gray
ISBN 978 1 84905 890 2
eISBN 978 0 85700 606 6

No Matter What
An Adoptive Family's Story of Hope, Love and Healing
Sally Donovan
ISBN 978 1 84905 431 7
eISBN 978 0 85700 781 0

Adoption is a Family Affair!
What Relatives and Friends Must Know
Patricia Irwin Johnston
ISBN 978 1 84905 895 7
eISBN 978 0 85700 619 6

Reparenting the Child Who Hurts
A Guide to Healing Developmental Trauma and Attachments
Caroline Archer and Christine Gordon
ISBN 978 1 84905 263 4
eISBN 978 0 85700 568 7

Attachment in Common Sense and Doodles
A Practical Guide
Miriam Silver
ISBN 978 1 84905 314 3
eISBN 978 0 85700 624 0

Preparing for Adoption

Everything Adopting Parents
Need to Know about Preparations,
Introductions and the First Few Weeks

Julia Davis
Foreword by Hugh Thornbery

Jessica Kingsley *Publishers*
London and Philadelphia

First published in 2015
by Jessica Kingsley Publishers
73 Collier Street
London N1 9BE, UK
and
400 Market Street, Suite 400
Philadelphia, PA 19106, USA

www.jkp.com

Library of Congress Cataloging in Publication Data
Davis, Julia, 1962-
Preparing for adoption : everything adopting parents need to know about preparations,
introductions and the first few weeks / Julia Davis ; foreword by Hugh Thornbery.
pages cm
Includes bibliographical references and index.
ISBN 978-1-84905-456-0
1. Adoption--Psychological aspects. 2. Adoptive parents. I. Title.
HV875.D353 2014
649'.145--dc23
2014013585

British Library Cataloguing in Publication Data
A CIP catalogue record for this book is available from the British Library

ISBN 978 1 84905 456 0
eISBN 978 085700 831 2

Printed and bound in Great Britain

For My Family

Contents

Foreword

This book is published at a significant time in the development of adoption in the UK. Each of the four constituent nations is addressing issues of adoption and permanence and while the focus of reform varies from nation to nation, the consistent underpinning driver is to ensure that children who can no longer live with their birth parents are found the right form of permanence as quickly as possible. Permanence can take many forms, and we have seen the development of different legal options over the last decade or so. Policy makers are quick to state that there is no hierarchy of preferred permanence options, and only the minority of children who enter the care system will end up being adopted, but there is no denying that an adoption order is a significant and hugely important transition in a child's life – legally transferring, forever, all the rights and responsibilities formerly held by the birth parents to the adoptive parents.

I believe that adoption is transformative for children. It provides a security and locus for life for the child. In the UK, the majority of adopted children are adopted from care. Over two-thirds of these children will have experienced traumatic starts to their lives before their entry into care. Some will have experienced more than one foster placement before being adopted. None of them will have had the continuity of parenting, love and care that all children should and need to have.

That is why this book by Julia Davis is so important. It comes at a time when we are seeking to find more adoptive placements for children in care. Consequently, we are experiencing changes to the law, regulations, processes and structures to support that ambition. In all of this change though, some things remain constant, and while the processes that prospective adopters go through have developed over time, the basic stages of consideration, preparation and decision-making have remained the same. Getting it right from the beginning is so important and this is where this book comes in.

Prospective adopters come to a decision to adopt through different motivations but all have to face the same fundamental issues of preparation. We know from recent research in England that the experience and issues faced by individual adoptive families will vary in nature and intensity: some adoptions will be plain sailing, others will be, at times, highly challenging. In all cases the greater the level of preparation and knowledge, the better placed adoptive parents will be to deal with the joys and sometime challenges of adopting a child who has had a very difficult start in life.

There is a wealth of advice from adopters and professionals available to prospective adopters and there is a growing body of evidence from academic research. Navigating all of this can be difficult at times but this new book will provide a significant leg up for those looking for clear information, practical advice and links to the research evidence.

The book is broken down into chapters that take the reader from an understanding of attachment, loss and trauma and the impact of these experiences on the development of the child's brain through to different stages of the adopter's preparation for the arrival of the child and the initial stages of placement. The strength of this book lies in its clear approach, setting out, at each stage of the process, what the adopter should know and expect, references to the relevant research, the roles and responsibilities of the professionals and excellent case studies that elaborate Julia Davis' points.

All of this is presented in a way that does not minimise the challenge that some adopters may face. It comes from a deep professional understanding that adopters want and need the right information, at the right time, presented in a straightforward way with the right professional support alongside them. The author also understands the thirst that adopters have for reading around the subject and becoming experts in all aspects of attachment, trauma and therapeutic parenting. To this end the book concludes with a detailed Bibliography and a recommended children's book list.

I believe that this book is a must-read for every prospective and new adopter: it is a good text for new entrants to adoption and fostering social work, and those with greater levels of knowledge will find it an invaluable reference resource. I hope you enjoy reading it as much as I did.

Hugh Thornbery
Chief Executive, Adoption UK
1 June 2014

Acknowledgements

I would like to thank all the children and families who have shared their experiences and stories with me. In particular I would like to thank Rachel, Ali, Kim, Marcie, Nicky, Elaine and Helen for sharing their stories of introductions. I would also like to thank Tracey for sharing her ideas and experiences as a foster carer.

I would like to acknowledge the colleagues I have worked with over the years who have shared their wisdom and experience with me as we have endeavoured to create good support services for children and their families – in particular I would like to thank those in the post-adoption team in Coventry: Laura, Karen, Jane, Sarah, Rachel and Amanda, as well as my colleagues at Adoptionplus. I would like to thank my managers, Pat and Gail, for supporting my quest to become a play therapist and encouraging me to keep going despite all the challenges we face in the work we do. I would also like to thank my supervisor, Nicki, for the support she has given me over the years in developing my practice.

Finally, I would like to say thank you to my family and friends – to my friends for their time to talk things over and patience when I have been too busy to meet; to my mother and father for their encouragement; to my sister for her editing and support for my ideas; to my children Ciaran, Eloise and Laurie who have continued to be wonderful even when I have been preoccupied with writing; and to my husband Peter, for his unfailing support.

Disclaimer/Note on the Text

I have addressed this book directly to adopters, but I hope that others will read it and find it useful – social workers, foster carers and support workers who are involved in a child's journey to adoption. I have written directly to adopters in the first person but recognise that you may be single or in a relationship. All the stories I have included are a mix of lots of different stories and all the identities have been changed.

About Adoptionplus and the Approach of this Book

Adoptionplus is a voluntary adoption agency, which was registered in 2008 to find families for older, harder-to-place children with complex needs. It offers an adoption service which places an emphasis on responsive adoption support and therapeutic practice. It employs a therapy team as part of its placement service, which is available to families when they need support led by a clinical child psychologist, and it offers a range of trauma and attachment-based therapies. The agency's philosophy is to ensure that children placed for adoption not only have secure, loving and happy homes, but also have the opportunity to heal from their early trauma, learn how to have relationships, manage their feelings and live satisfying lives.

The agency works with children to help them develop a coherent sense of their past, an understanding of what had happened and why it may have happened. Many children often believe that it is their fault that their birth parents could not look after them, or abused and hurt them. They think that they are unlovable or bad and that they are responsible for all of the pain they have suffered. Leaving children with these distorted self-beliefs not only negatively affects the development of new, healthy attachment relationships with their adoptive or foster parents, but is also likely to lead to a life of ongoing emotional pain. They often feel unable to gain the comfort and support of healthy emotional relationships with others, as it is difficult for them to believe that they are lovable, it becomes difficult for them to trust that other people genuinely care for them. Additionally, children may have a distorted view of their birth parents. They may attribute positive qualities to them that do not exist. In turn, these fantasies can hinder the development of healthy attachment relationships with their adoptive parents. Contact is a key element in the work of Adoptionplus as it provides an opportunity to clarify the myths and promote a realistic and helpful understanding of past events. Seeing for themselves and understanding why their parents may have behaved as they did can correct children's distorted self-beliefs, and this is enormously important for long-term emotional health.

Adoptionplus also works with birth parents who have had their children removed and placed for adoption. These parents are often confused about how they have ended up in this situation, let alone what to say to their children about it. Many birth parents welcome support and guidance to aid them in helping their children. With the right support, some parents are keen to apologise for mistakes they have made and explain to their children that none of it was their fault; this can also be beneficial for the birth parents' emotional health. Their sense of self-worth can increase if they can feel that they are offering their child something that is helpful to them. Offering some feeling of resolution is better than the pain of none at all. This pain can often leave birth parents stuck in the trauma of losing their children and make it very difficult for them to move forward in their lives, and can in fact lead to further deterioration in emotional health.

The more emotionally healthy the birth parents feel, the better it is for their children. In the current age of Facebook and the Internet, there are clear benefits in investing in addressing unresolved issues as early as possible. Local authorities already spend resources on the area of contact, but this investment could be much more beneficial if contact is treated not just as a space where resources are used to monitor and assess, but to benefit significantly the emotional health of both the children and their birth parents.

Introduction

When I first started working with children, I used to take a bag of toys and some colouring pens and paper with me on my visits. I was keen to help the children on my caseload communicate what they were thinking and feeling about being in care. I wanted to help them make sense of their experiences and settle in their new families. We would sit and share their stories and try to understand what had happened. I would sit with their foster carers and adopters over a cup of tea and we would try to make sense of the things the children were struggling with – nightmares, fighting with their siblings, refusing to do as they were told or getting into trouble at school. What we needed to help us understand their struggles was the body of knowledge that has developed in recent years about attachment and the impact of trauma on children.

The research into attachment and trauma gives us a framework to help us make sense of what we see, understand behaviours and identify ways to support you and your children to create positive ways of living together. By using this framework to think about introductions in adoption, we can identify ways to shape the process to take account of your children's early experiences and their need for attachment-based parenting. The framework can shape the preparations that are made and the early days of family life. It will help you to understand the struggles your children may have when moving to live with you and give you ideas to support your parenting in an attachment-focused way.

How do you make sense of your child's behaviour? How should you understand the impact on them of their early experiences of neglect and abuse? How can you help them recover from these experiences and form good attachment relationships with you? Chapter One discusses ideas about attachment theory, trauma and loss to begin to answer these questions. Chapter Two considers the impact of adverse experiences on a child's brain and development and it creates a framework of knowledge to inform the process of introductions. This framework will shape the rest of the book as the various aspects of the process of introductions are discussed in terms of attachment and trauma.

Chapter Three focuses on the preparations you will make – on the information you need to gain from the foster carer and on preparing your home and information for your child from an attachment perspective. It also considers the preparation you need to do as an individual, by exploring your own attachment history.

Chapter Four discusses how to prepare your family and friends so they can support you. Ideas about how to prepare your own children and the children in your extended family are discussed, for example, by exploring their feelings about a new child joining their family and the issues your new child's history may raise for them. Preparing your family to support you as you parent from an attachment perspective is also discussed – the difficulties that you might encounter are considered, as well as ways to involve your family in the process.

Chapter Five discusses how to prepare a child to move to an adoptive family. It looks at the life-story work that is needed, how to support a child to mourn the losses they will experience and how to prepare them to move to a new family. This chapter also gives you ideas about how to continue your child's story once they are living with you.

Chapter Six focuses on the actual days of introductions and how to shape them from an attachment perspective. The plans, timescales and people involved are all considered in the context of helping a child form new attachment relationships while acknowledging the value of the relationships they are leaving. Some of the challenges that you might encounter and ways to help the process go smoothly are discussed.

Chapter Seven explores how to create a safe, attachment-focused family life once your child has come to live with you. It focuses on what to do and how to do it in the very early days of becoming a family. There are ideas on what to play and how to look after your children and the emphasis is on attachment-based parenting.

Chapter Eight considers some of the challenges you might face and how to manage them. It explores some of the times during the day which might be stressful and some of the challenges you may encounter in parenting children who have experienced early trauma. It also considers some of the emotional challenges you may face as an adopter and what may help you manage these.

CHAPTER ONE

● ● ● ● ● ● ● ● ● ● ●

Making Sense of it All

Introduction

John and Sally met Libby at her foster carer's home when Libby was three years old. From the very first minute she called them 'mummy' and 'daddy' and she was keen to sit on her new daddy's lap and play with her new toys. When they took her out to the park, she insisted on holding daddy's hand and walking all the way, rather than going in her pushchair. While they were at the park, she fell off the swing but did not cry and shrugged off their efforts to comfort her. Back at the foster carer's, Sally tried to give Libby her tea but she refused to eat, asking for John to feed her. While playing with her new toy, she bumped her finger and made a huge fuss so everyone came to see what was the matter. When bath-time came, she insisted on showing them how clever she was at getting herself ready and resisted their efforts to help her put her nightdress on. Once Libby had moved to live with John and Sally, she continued to rebuff Sally's efforts to take care of her. If they had visitors Libby would be charming and playful, as long as she was in charge of the game. If she needed anything, she would approach any adult in the room rather than seek Sally out, and she would push Sally away if she tried to give her a cuddle.

David was four years old when Sue and Peter met him at his foster carer's. He hid behind his foster carer when they came to the front door and he stayed close to her as Sue and Peter tried to engage him in playing with the game they had brought him. Over the next few days, Sue and Peter took turns to give David his tea, bathe him and they took him to the park together to feed the ducks. When they were out, David kept asking where his foster carer was, looking for her each time they came back from the park. On the day of his move, David got into the car without a fuss, sitting quietly in the car all the way to Sue and Peter's house and letting Sue take his hand to take him inside. Over the next few weeks, David seemed to settle well; he ate all his meals, played with his toys and slept through the night. He rarely cried or made a fuss and did not seek cuddles from either Sue or Peter, although he was happy enough to let them pick him up. However, one day Sue said it was time for tea so they would not be going to watch television, and he had a huge temper tantrum followed by lots of tears. At the meeting to review how things were going, he went up to the reviewing officer and called her mummy and asked her to play with him.

What is happening in these stories about introductions and how can we make sense of them? There are common themes in each story about a child moving to live with an adoptive family: this book will consider such themes to help you begin to make sense of your own adoption story. Some of the questions this book will explore include how to understand the effects of past experiences on your child. How can you make sense of their behaviour? How can you best prepare yourself to parent them? Your child may have lived in several families, experienced the loss of their birth parents and siblings and lived through things which were hurtful and frightening before they came to live with you. How can you make sense of this, for them and for you?

This chapter will explore ideas about attachment, loss and trauma to help you make sense of your child's experiences and the impact of them on their well-being and development. It will help you understand their behaviour, the struggles they may be undergoing and give you ideas about how to shape your parenting to help them thrive. The ideas in this chapter will complement the training and reading you have done as part of your assessment. As adopters, you will have your own life experiences and ideas which will shape your template for family life. In preparation groups when issues were raised, you may have thought 'that won't happen to my child, we will do it differently', or, 'that won't apply to my child, they were only tiny when they went into foster care'. You may feel preoccupied with becoming a family, having waited so long. Sometimes the more theoretical ideas you have learnt will only seem relevant once you are living at home with your adopted child.

Every child's experience is unique; some come into care as a baby, others after years of living with their birth family; they might live with a lovely foster carer, or they might have stayed with several carers without having good relationships with them; they may have experienced physical or sexual abuse, neglect or exposure to domestic violence; they may have experienced the pain of separation from people they were attached to and they have all lost their birth family. Their experience remains unique to them, but understanding the theoretical ideas will help you develop a parenting approach that will help your child settle well, whatever their individual experience.

Attachment

One of the most important goals you will have as a new adoptive parent is to develop a secure attachment with your child. In order to achieve this, you need to have a sense of both your child's and your own attachment patterns. Gray (2012b) highlights how, on moving in, children will often behave as they did in their first home – using the attachment patterns formed in their early interactions with their birth parents. You might find your child is overly controlling or self-reliant at first – they may resist your attempts to look after them and want to do everything for themselves and do it their way, not your way. You might find them extremely clingy, following you everywhere and making a big fuss over the smallest setback. Ideas from the field of attachment theory will help you understand their attachment behaviours, make sense of what you are experiencing with them and give you a framework within which to build a secure attachment relationship with them.

Attachment theory explains a child's development within the context of their relationships. How they experience the world and their relationships in it will affect their development in all areas – physical, behavioural, emotional, social and intellectual. With a positive, secure attachment a child will develop positive social and emotional relationships, learn well and develop good social skills. They will develop an internal working model of the world (Bowlby 1998) based on their experience of sensitive and attuned care. They will learn that they are valued for themselves and that their needs will be met in a positive way. They will learn to trust their feelings and how they make sense of the world, they will feel they can make things happen or can find an adult to help them if they need it, they will develop a complex vocabulary of emotions and they will be able to communicate their emotions and be able to respond to stress appropriately (Van der Kolk 2005).

A child with secure attachment will develop a sense of confidence in the care they receive and a sense of their own self-worth. If they need help or are upset, they will seek out their parent to make them feel better. They will also develop a sense of their parent as their secure base so they can venture out into the world and start exploring, confident that their parent is there to return to if they need them. Children who can play confidently are quickly soothed by their parent when they are cross or upset, and children who seek contact with their parent when they have been apart demonstrate a secure attachment relationship with that parent.

Secure attachment

How is this achieved? Howe (2005) has described attachment as necessary for survival – for a helpless baby, the attachment process is designed to ensure the attachment figure stays close, thereby keeping the baby alive and safe. When the baby shows distress, usually by crying, their attachment figure – mother, father or carer – sees their distress, meets their need and calms them – whether they are wet, hungry, bored or cold. Over time, with many repeated interactions between them, a secure attachment pattern develops as the baby's needs are consistently met and their distress is soothed in a timely and appropriate way.

There are several elements essential in creating such a secure attachment pattern:

- The parent needs to be able to attune to the baby's emotional state and recognise and regulate their feelings. If the baby is crying, they should be able to work out what is the matter rather than always assuming they are hungry and giving them a bottle to stop them crying.

- The parent needs to have positive interactions with the baby using facial expressions, eye contact, tone of voice (its pitch and rhythm) and touch. A gentle singsong voice and a smiling face, accompanied by rocking the baby to and fro, create a positive connection (rather than a harsh voice and rough handling).

- The parent needs to be able to see the baby as its own person, with its own feelings and personality. They should be curious about how their baby is feeling and how it might be experiencing the world, rather than imposing their own view.

- The parent needs to be able to reflect accurately what the baby is feeling. Rather than showing an angry or irritated face when the baby is crying the parent might show a sad face.

- If the baby is upset, the parent is able to soothe them and calm their strong emotions. So if the baby cries, the parent will rock them and sing to them rather than shouting at them to stop crying.

- The parent is able to take turns in their interaction with their baby rather than dominating the interaction. So in playing games like peekaboo, each can take a turn and the baby can turn away when they have had enough.

- The baby has just a small number of people that take care of them so they can develop special relationships rather than many that are superficial. If they are in special care, the hospital will try to use key nurses to avoid just anyone on shift caring for that baby. (Gray 2012b; Howe 2005; Siegel and Hartzell 2004)

You can use all these ideas in establishing your relationship with your child when they come to live with you. This will help build your secure attachment with them.

Attachment as a process starts at birth and continues throughout childhood and adolescence. At birth a newborn seeks care and protection through closeness to their carer. The baby is aware of the way their needs are met and can distinguish between the parent smiling or frowning when they pick them up. By three months the baby is more selective and will focus on specific people, smiling less readily at strangers. By six months the baby shows a clear preference for their attachment figure – their parent – and will begin to show anxiety and distress when they are separated and be less tolerant of being held by strangers. As they develop, they will show a strong preference for their attachment figure and will begin to use them as a secure base from which to explore their world. Between two and four years of age they will become more self-reliant and better able to cope with periods of separation from their attachment figure. They will start to communicate their emotions and be able to use their parent for reassurance and comfort. As they grow older and enter adolescence, their attachment needs will lessen as they become more independent – however, even during this period they still have a strong need for their attachment figure, to give them the security and confidence to manage their developing independence (Golding 2008).

Understanding your child's developmental stages and the significance of their attachment figure is key to making sense of their behaviour as they join your family. Think about how old they are when they move and who has been their attachment figure.

With sensitive, loving, consistent, responsive, available and accepting care, the child will develop a secure attachment pattern. They may not receive this kind of care every minute of every day, as every parent has off days – but it would be their experience as a general rule. Their internal working model will be that they are lovable and valued and that others are good and available to help them. They will carry this model as they grow up and it will shape their future relationships and their openness to learning and to new experiences. They will carry a positive sense of their own self-worth and an expectation of a positive future for themselves (Howe 2005).

This is the kind of attachment relationship you will want to create with your adoptive child – but they may have developed very different attachment patterns with their birth parents, and this will affect the building of attachment relationships with you.

What happens if your child has had insensitive parenting that was not as loving, consistent or responsive? Your child may feel anxious about where you are and may not be confident that you will stay with them or look after them. They may feel uncertain about the reaction they will get from you when they need looking after. They may then follow an insecure attachment pattern rather than a secure one.

Insecure attachment patterns

If a parent cannot give their child consistent and attuned parenting, this will have a significant impact on their child's development of an attachment pattern and the child will develop insecure attachment patterns. Through their relationship with their parent, the child learns how to regulate their own behaviour, as they anticipate their parent's response. They need to stay close to their parent to have their needs met and ensure their survival – they will adapt to the kind of parenting they are given. Disruption in the development of a secure attachment pattern may happen due to experiences you may recognise as part of your child's history. These include living with a parent suffering from chronic depression or who is addicted to drugs or alcohol, experiencing abuse or neglect at home, sudden separation from a parent (by death, illness or going into care), frequent moves or placements and inconsistent or inadequate care (Howe 2005; Golding 2008).

There are different kinds of insecure attachment patterns – insecure ambivalent, anxious avoidant and disorganised – when the parent does not offer consistent, attuned care, but their parenting is shaped by their own emotional difficulties. The child adapts their response to the parent as a result.

Insecure ambivalent attachment pattern:
When the parent is inconsistent

Parents may be preoccupied by their own emotional issues and be unreliable and emotionally neglectful. Sometimes they will give the child a bottle, at other times they may forget or not feel bothered. Sometimes they will be playful and comforting, at others they will be distant and absent. The child never knows what to expect and fears that their parent will disappear. They do not trust that their parent will come back if they go away and they cannot trust that they will meet their needs. The child may swing between being clingy and pushing their parent away – when they come back after being away, the child may fail to settle and keep crying, unsure whether to go to their parent or to stay away from them. Their parent has been unpredictable and neglectful, so the child becomes clingy and demanding – they want to get their parent's attention and keep it. However, if they show that they are all right, then their parent might forget them again so they keep on demanding that they look after them. They are hard to soothe and fuss over the smallest of things. Their internal working model is a world where the parent is uninterested in them, unreliable and unavailable and that the child themself is unlovable (Golding 2008; Gray 2012b).

Libby, the girl in the introduction, had lived in a house where there was chaos and domestic violence. Her mother was addicted to drugs and alcohol and her parenting of Libby was extremely erratic; when she was sober she remembered to feed her, but when she was drunk her child was forgotten. Libby had survived in a house of unsafe adults where she had to make sure her needs were met by charming the adults around her. If they didn't notice her then she would not be fed. She lived in a frightening environment with no one to make sure she was safe.

She developed an insecure, ambivalent attachment pattern as a result of these early experiences with her birth mother – when she moved to live with her new adoptive parents she behaved with them as if they were offering her the same insecure parenting. She was controlling of them and her friends to help her feel safe, she would alternate between pushing them away and demanding their attention to ensure they noticed her, and she would make the biggest fuss over the smallest thing to ensure she was not forgotten.

Anxious avoidant attachment pattern: When the parent is hostile, controlling and rejecting

If their child is distressed, they are unresponsive and resentful. They may shout and be unkind. They may find their child's needs overwhelming and withdraw, leaving them to cry.

The child responds by overregulating their own emotions — if they show a need, emotion or vulnerability they risk driving their parent away and then they will not be looked after. The child can seem passive and withdrawn or extremely compliant. They act as if they do not need a parent. Their internal working model is one where the adult is hostile, intrusive and unresponsive and that the children are unlovable. This child may make no fuss if they are hurt and behave as if they can look after themselves (Golding 2008; Gray 2012b).

David, the boy in the introduction, had lived with his birth mother for the first two years of his life. She had a history of mental illness and struggled to look after David. When she was depressed, she would leave him in his cot for long periods of time. Even if he cried loudly she did not go to find out what he needed. Sometimes she would pick him up and shout at him for crying and making such a noise. So after a while, he cried less. As he became a toddler, he learnt not to make a fuss or a noise as this would make his mother angry or upset and she would cry. When he was hungry, he would wait and wait to be fed but he could not make a fuss because she would be angry again. David developed an insecure avoidant pattern of attachment as a result of his experiences of living with his birth mother. He could not show his needs as he feared what the response from his parent would be. When he moved to live with his adoptive parents, he responded in the same way with them — he could not trust that they would meet his needs and he feared their response if he showed any vulnerability so he was obedient and compliant on moving in.

*Disorganised pattern of attachment: When the parent
is frightening, dangerous or frightened themselves*

The parent cannot keep the child safe – the child may be exposed
to scary situations such as domestic violence or they may actually
hurt the child. The parent cannot regulate a stressful situation for
their child as they themselves are unable to manage stress and
are a part of the situation. The child needs to seek comfort –
but the very person who should comfort them is also the cause
of their distress – so they feel helpless and confused. They do
not know whether they will get a cuddle or a smack, as these
are given by the same person. The child's level of distress stays
high and they are not able to develop a good way of organising
their behaviour in response to their own parent. The child can
be tearful and aggressive – feeling angry with the person who
should be caring for them, but terrified of them at the same time.
The child may become increasingly controlling in an attempt to
try and predict what will happen to them and to keep themselves
safe. The child may struggle with being close to someone and
find it hard to be soothed, as they cannot trust their response. In
their internal working model, they are unlovable and bad, and
the parent is frightening, unavailabe and not to be trusted (Gray
2012b; Golding 2008).

Understanding these types of attachment patterns and how
they affect a child's interactions and the way in which they make
sense of their world can help you make sense of the way your
child relates to you, and the impact of their early relationships on
their attachment behaviours. We have all developed attachment
patterns which span a range from insecure to secure attachment,
depending on our own childhood experiences. Thinking about
your own attachment history can be helpful when preparing to
become a parent, so you can recognise your own attachment
behaviour and how it affects your interactions with your child.
You do not need to have had the perfect childhood, but you
do need to be able to reflect on your own history in a way that
makes sense of it and resolves any difficulties that did occur. It is
helpful to be able to identify your own attachment pattern and
how you behave as a consequence, particularly when you are

under stress. Consider this to be an essential part of the process of becoming an adoptive parent, as it will affect your forming an attachment with your adopted child (Siegel and Hartzell 2004).

Find out about your child's history and the early care they received – ask how they were cared for and how many carers they had. Explore with your social worker the kind of parenting their birth parents had and the experiences they struggled with which will have shaped their own parenting and attachment patterns. This will help you to construct a picture of your child's early attachment patterns and their internal working model of the world. Ask their foster carer what they have noticed – do they describe their behaviour in ways that fit with some of the attachment patterns we have looked at? In the early weeks when they move in with you, keep these models in your head to help you to identify their attachment patterns.

Notice how they show their needs and how they respond to your attempts to meet these needs. Notice how they respond when they are hurt, tired or upset – do they seek you out and accept your care, or do they try to look after themselves or look to their brother or sister to take care of them? They will shape their behaviour in relation to what they expect to happen – they will carry their model of attachment behaviour into your family and behave in the way they have relied on to survive so far. Your challenge will be to change that model and their expectations of you as their parent and how you will behave towards them. They may worry that you won't be there consistently or may go away and not come back; they may worry that you won't see their needs as important and that you may be cross and scary when they do something wrong; they may even worry you will hurt them if that has been their past experience. They may feel that they are not worth worrying or caring about and that they are not lovable. It may be that, in their eyes, anyone will do to look after them and they may feel puzzled or threatened by your attempts to get close to them.

Even if they have received great care from their foster carers they will carry the profound impact of their early experiences in their birth family. How their early experiences affect them is the complex result of their genetic inheritance, their own personality and their environment, in particular their relationships. This is one of the most difficult parts of the picture to figure out – your child will be affected to a greater or lesser degree, depending on all these factors. You, as their adoptive parent, will form a hugely significant part of the picture and how it looks when it is completed. By giving them care which is safe, reliable and consistent, over time they will create a new internal working model which reflects these different relationships and the attachment between you (Golding 2008).

Loss and trauma

Loss

Even tiny babies are affected by their early experiences – they will have experienced the loss of their birth mother and may have had many different carers in hospital. Verrier argues that this first loss has a profound impact on the adopted child and they need to be allowed to grieve to enable them to fully engage with their adopted family (Verrier 1993).

Understanding the impact of separation and loss on your child is another essential piece of the picture. Each child joining an adoptive family will experience loss – of their birth parents and siblings, their foster carers and their families, their familiar home, belongings, neighbourhood, school and friends. The shadows of their separation from their birth family can linger over the separation from their foster family and create an even more complex sense of loss for the child, as all their experiences of loss become intertwined. As their adoptive parent, you need to acknowledge and understand the impact of these losses on your child, and support them in grieving those losses so they are able to resolve their sense of loss and be better able to begin forming new attachments with you. This can be a challenge as it is in contrast to your own excitement and joy at becoming a family.

Adult grieving follows a pattern of shock, denial, anger, bargaining, sadness and acceptance (Kübler–Ross 1969).

Children also experience these emotions, but not in such a linear sequential pattern. They are more likely to stop and start in their grieving – Di Stubbs from Winston's Wish Charity has described it as like jumping in and out of puddles – but they need support to come to terms with their loss (Stubbs *et al.* 2009). They might feel sad to be leaving their foster carer and angry that they have to move; they may feel a huge sense of shock as they realise the enormity of leaving behind all their friends and familiar life; they may feel a sense of guilt that, somehow, they caused all this to happen.

Think about their behaviour during introductions from a grief and loss perspective:

- They may leave foster care without a backward glance and play happily with their toys on the first day with you – looking as if they have settled well and aren't sad at all. They may be shocked and in denial that this move is permanent.

- They may have tantrums or sulk. They may be angry at the change in their life over which they had no say.

- They may appear eager to please you, or alternatively they may try to get themselves sent back to their foster carer. They may try to bargain with you to get what they want, for example, to return to their foster carer.

- They may seem anxious, have no energy or enthusiasm for anything, or feel they can't do anything. They may be feeling sad about their loss.

- After a while, they may seem more energetic and engaged with you. They may be more accepting of this new situation.

The age of your child when they move and their developmental stage will also affect their sense of loss. Very young babies rely on sensory experience to make sense of their world and are vulnerable to changes they can't as yet understand. Young children have not developed the capacity to think as an adult, so they may see the move as their fault, because of something they have done or because they see themselves as a bad child. They may not understand the reason why they are being adopted and are leaving their foster carer, so may create their own explanation that they were kidnapped, bought or stolen. If they have moved several times before, then they may want to protect themselves from the pain of another separation and the loss of another relationship. This may cause them to become emotionally detached from the process (Fahlberg 2012, Gray 2012b).

Some social workers suggest that if a child has made a good attachment relationship with their foster carer, they are capable of transferring this to their adopter. While your child may have the ability to make another attachment, the pain of losing the first one needs to be acknowledged – the closer they were, the longer they were with them, the more it is going to hurt to move and the more they will need support to grieve this loss. Adoptive parents can sometimes feel they are getting it wrong and they can't connect with their child – but it may be that their child has put up a barrier against getting hurt again and is scared of making a new relationship. As an adoptive parent, you are trying to support a child that has lost the person they love and trust, while you are trying to start creating a relationship of love and trust with them – they are in the middle, which increases their emotional vulnerability during the early days of an adoption.

For a child to grieve and move on with a sense of having resolved their loss, they need support from adults to help them to share feelings about their loss. This mirrors aspects of a secure attachment relationship. As an adoptive parent, you will be able to give these to your child while acknowledging that these are the very things they may have lost as they left their foster carer (Gray 2012b).

Trauma

A child placed for adoption may have experienced living in a home that was dirty and chaotic, where they were left hungry and cold, where their parents did not keep them safe and where they may have been exposed to drug and alcohol addiction, domestic violence and frightening scenes between the grown-ups. Their parents may have hurt them in different ways – physically, sexually and emotionally. Van der Kolk's (2005) model of developmental trauma helps us understand the impact of growing up in a family where these experiences are a daily occurrence. Developmental trauma is not focused on the impact of an isolated traumatic incident, such as a car crash, but on a child's experience of chronic repeated trauma – where they are exposed to multiple and prolonged developmentally adverse traumatic events, starting in their very early childhood and in their family relationships.

Van der Kolk (2005) describes how such trauma will have a complicated effect on a child's development in all areas:

- They may develop an unfocused response to stress.

- They may struggle to regulate their emotions.

- They may lack a sense of cause and effect.

- They may lack a sense of predictability or reliability in people or events.

- They may see anything new as a potential threat.

- They may struggle to make sense of events.

When a child has been exposed to chronic trauma, they may have intense emotional responses to minor events – they may feel shame, rage and fear when there seems no logical trigger for these intense feelings. They can be overreactive and misinterpret events – they expect the world to be bad and to hurt them and they fear abandonment.

Their experience of chronic trauma, when they have not been cared for and have been hurt by the very people who should have been protecting and looking after them, will have affected how they think, feel and behave. Their attachment relationships and their internal working model will also have been affected by their experience of developmental trauma. They have experienced adults as threatening and frightening towards them. They have developed responses to try to minimise their sense of threat and manage their feelings of distress and fear.

The child's reactions may also be triggered by reminders of traumatic events and they may react with a stress response seemingly unrelated to the actual event – a teacher's tone of voice may trigger a memory of a parent shouting at them, or a football coach raising his or her arm may trigger a memory of someone lifting their arm to hit them. Sensory triggers, such as the smell of urine or aftershave, can also bring back the feelings of fear and helplessness they had when they were abused. They may behave as if they were under threat again – reacting with fight, flight or freeze responses which the person in front of them may struggle to understand if they do not know and bear in mind that this child has experienced developmental trauma.

As an adopter, the challenge is to understand why your child is misinterpreting what is happening and what has led to their emotional response. Try to think about what your child has experienced and how this has affected them. Sometimes the words 'trauma' and 'traumatised' are used too glibly, but when applied to your child's experience, they help you begin to understand the profound impact this experience has had on their development and sense of the world. As their parent, you can offer them ways to recover from these experiences by creating a safe home in which they can make new connections with you as safe adults caring for them (Gray 2012a).

To help a child recover from their history of trauma, Van der Kolk identifies certain key elements – that the child needs to develop a sense of mastery of themselves, be able to regulate their emotions appropriately and experience a sense of calm and safety, where the adult is in charge and keeps them safe (Van der

Kolk 2005). A child can recover and heal when they are looked after in a safe home, where they can develop secure attachment relationships and be able to express in words or play what has happened to them. An adoptive home which is shaped to meet the needs of a child who has experienced developmental trauma will have:

- safety, with a high level of structure and supervision

- predictability, with a clear routine

- parents who are reliable and consistent

- parents who offer lots of nurture

- opportunities to have fun and experience positive emotions

- opportunities to play and talk about their past and their worries

- opportunities to try new things and develop a sense of mastery

- an environment which protects them from trauma triggers.

If you give your child such a home, it will give them the opportunity to recover from the impact on their development of their early experiences of trauma (Perry *et al.* 1995, 2006; Golding 2008).

CHAPTER TWO

● ● ● ● ● ● ● ● ● ●

Other Ideas to Consider

Placing your child's experience within the context of ideas about attachment, loss and trauma creates a framework with which to shape your parenting and the pattern of introductions.

Further elements of this framework stem from ideas about the brain, sensory integration and Hughes and Baylin's model of attachment-focused parenting (Hughes and Baylin 2012).

Consider the brain

Research into the functions of the brain and how it develops plays a critical part in informing our understanding of how children develop and how this development is affected by a child's experiences. The research considers how a child's experience of their environment and relationships, particularly in the first three years of life, affects the development of the brain, which in turn impacts on the child's development.

Brain structure – how it develops

At birth, a child's brain is an immature organ; its growth will be determined by a complex combination of factors: genetics, prenatal factors and the child's environment and relationships. The nerve cells in the brain – neurons – need to develop connections – called synapses – to enable the brain to function. With positive experiences, the brain develops a richer network of connections; conversely, with negative experiences, fewer neural connections are developed. Gerhardt describes in *Why Love Matters* (Gerhardt 2004) the critical importance of this concept in the development of a child's brain – the more neural connections, the better the brain will function. The brain is described as having 'plasticity', i.e. the brain is able to change its response to repeated stimulation. Synaptic connections are either strengthened or discarded over time, depending on whether they are used or not. The child's experiences are a crucial factor in determining which synapses are lost and which are strengthened. With less stimulation of these connections, there is a negative long-term impact on the child's social and cognitive development, learning, memory and speech development. The stark example of the Romanian orphans who were left in their cots without interaction with the adults responsible for their care shows the critical role a developing child's relationships play – parts of their brains simply did not develop due to the extreme neglect the orphans experienced (Gerhardt 2004; NSCDC 2009).

The brain has three parts which develop in a sequential pattern. The lower region is the brainstem, also called the reptilian brain. This governs bodily functions such as eating, breathing and movement. It activates instinctive behaviour related to survival – the fight, flight, freeze response is located here. This part of the brain is less susceptible to environmental factors. The middle region is called the limbic brain or emotional brain. This activates emotions and urges, such as feelings of fear or rage, and also helps control the primitive fight/flight responses to stress. The higher region of the brain is called the reflective, rational brain or cortex. It is the structure responsible for reason, planning, communication and reflection; where imagination, creativity and empathy are located. In the very early years of a child's life, the development of the limbic and cortex structures are ongoing – so the lower brain dominates in the early years, with the functions of the higher brain structures taking over critical roles as the brain matures. How these structures are shaped depends on the experiences the growing child receives – so they are termed experience-dependent, unlike the lower structures (Perry 2006; Siegel and Hartzell 2004; Sunderland 2006).

For optimal development of these structures, the child needs experiences which are safe, predictable, gradual, repetitive and attuned to their developmental state (Perry and Pollard 1997). With this kind of experience, the brain's architecture is shaped in the most positive way for the child to develop and thrive. Good connections are developed between the different structures of the brain so it is able to function well.

As an adoptive parent, you can shape your interactions with your child to offer them experiences to help them develop such good connections. They may have adapted to a negative environment before coming to you, when their interactions with their parents were unsafe, unpredictable and haphazard, but by offering them an environment and relationships that are safe, reliable and predictable you can help them develop a different developmental pathway. Rather than a harsh tone and rough handling with a baby, a gentle singsong tone of voice, gentle back and forth rocking and a smiling face are the kind of experiences they need. Older children need safe, consistent parenting with opportunities for sensory and rhythmic play with you, rather than being left to care for themselves in a chaotic home life.

Research shows that there is a huge growth in connections in the brain during the first three years of a child's life – but such research also highlights that growth continues throughout a child's life, with further episodes of significant development. Between the ages of three and five, there is major development in executive functioning – in the areas of inhibitory control, working memory and cognitive and mental flexibility. With these functions a child is able to retain information in the short-term, resist temptation and distraction, pause and think before they act and adjust to changes in demands and priorities. These are all crucial for entering school and, if they are not developed, they can have a negative effect on the child's learning and ability to interact socially. Your child might struggle to sit still in class and understand what the teacher is asking them to do, as they are too busy watching the other children at the next table. They might find it hard not to take a rubber from the table, even if it isn't theirs, just because it looks nice. Or they might find it hard to organise what they need to take for school the next day and then struggle to move between different lessons as the school day progresses. These are all aspects of executive functioning that they might need support with if their development in these areas was impaired by their early experiences (Bomber 2007).

The brain continues to develop right through to the mid-twenties as it adapts to its environment before it is mature – so even if your child comes to you as an older child, there are ongoing opportunities to affect how the architecture of their brain is shaped by the parenting you give them. Adolescence is another time of intense development in the brain with the onset of puberty. There is development in the areas which direct reasoning, impulse control, planning and emotional regulation – all of which are areas teenagers often need support in. Without the development of the more mature cortex and thinking skills, the teenager stays reliant on the emotions of the limbic brain – this can lead to them struggling to interpret emotions correctly and to putting themselves at risk as they lack the rational reflective skills to consider their behaviours and the possible consequences of their actions. Even as they are striving for independence, they need the support of a secure attachment figure to enable them to develop these functions successfully (Brown and Ward 2013; Golding 2008). This research highlights another opportunity for you as an adoptive parent to provide positive experiences which will have a direct impact on your growing teenager's brain in the future.

Response to stress

Thinking about the brain's function in relation to stress is important in understanding your child. Margot Sunderland (2006) describes how cells in the brain are activated by hormones and natural chemicals. She identifies oxytocin and opioids as playing an essential role in good child/parent relationships. These create a sense of well-being and are released and activated by the brain in response to warm, attuned parenting. A parent touching a child in a warm and gentle way, cuddling them and stroking their hair can activate the release of oxytocin and create a positive relationship. The more this happens, the more the sense of a positive relationship will develop between the parent and child (Sunderland 2006).

When a child is under stress and their parent is harmful or unresponsive

The brain's response to stress is immature at birth and the child's early experiences play a critical role in shaping their response to stress. In a secure attachment relationship, when the child is distressed the parent responds to their distress, soothes them, calms them and the stress is resolved. The child can't yet do this for themselves, so they need the experience of an adult attuned to their needs – if they are crying, their parent should pick them up, rock them and soothe them and then work out what they need and respond to this so they are no longer distressed. If they are left to cry and no one comes to pick them up or sort out what is the matter, they are left in an unresolved state of stress – this produces high levels of the stress hormone, cortisol. Too much cortisol is dangerous to the developing brain as it impairs its development (Perry and Pollard 1997; Siegel and Hartzell 2004; Sunderland 2006).

The child needs to develop a system to manage their response to stress – this can be any event which might threaten their well-being and survival. In everyday life they will need to learn how to manage varying levels of stress and be able to return themselves to a state of calm – this could be the stress of feeling hungry, starting at a new school or being told off. In the beginning they will depend on their carer being attuned to their needs and regulating their stress, and over time as they mature they will be able to self-regulate their own stress when their needs are unmet. So when they are thirsty as a baby they are dependent on a carer offering them a bottle and soothing their distress at being thirsty, when they are older they can feel thirsty, feel uncomfortable as a result but be able to ask for a drink or get themselves one to regulate their own feeling of distress at being thirsty.

The amygdala, located in the limbic brain, is a key filter for all sensory information and works out whether a situation is safe or threatening. If it identifies a situation as unsafe, it will trigger another part of the brain, the hypothalamus, to activate the release of cortisol. Its role is to focus the body on dealing with the stress, in order to survive. Once the threat has been dealt with, the systems restore balance and cortisol is no longer produced. A young child needs an adult to restore their sense of safety, by soothing and tending to them – they may pick them up, sing to them, feed them or rock them to calm them. As the child grows up they will have learnt from repeated experience with their parent how to respond appropriately when they are stressed to regulate their negative emotions. They will learn to seek out adults to look after them if they are upset, and, as they grow older, they will learn how to calm themselves and look after themselves as their thinking brain works out what is going on and how to react (Hughes and Baylin 2012; Siegel and Hartzell 2004).

If their parent is hostile, neglectful or angry, or if they are in a stressful environment, such as living with parents who fight, then they are constantly exposed to stress. When the child experiences chronic, unrelieved stress, they have very high levels of cortisol – or in some cases very low levels. The child develops an abnormal response to stress. The child is less able to deal with the stress they encounter in everyday life and struggles to manage their emotions. They may overreact to minor stresses, be impulsive, and struggle to learn or to develop their social skills.

They may find any new situation, even if it is meant to be fun, potentially threatening and hard to manage, as they lack the capacity to manage the stress it involves.

Although you may plan a trip to the zoo as a treat, they may struggle to enjoy the outing as they are triggered by the newness of the place and the strangeness of the experience into feeling threatened. If they have lived with you for a short while, they may not yet be able to rely on you to keep them safe and soothe their distress and so will struggle on their own to manage their feelings. This may result in meltdowns and tantrums rather than the excitement and the fun you had envisaged (Perry 2009).

Fight/flight/freeze response

The signal to the brain of a threat will trigger the survival system located in the lower brain – and this will prepare the body for a fight/flight/freeze response in order to survive the perceived threat. A child faced with an angry neighbour and a broken window may either run back to his mother (flight), start shouting that it wasn't his fault (fight) or stand rooted to the spot, unable to move or say anything (freeze). They need calming to restore their sense of safety, so the arrival of their mother to sort things out will calm them and enable them to resolve the threat. In babies, a state of alarm is more likely to trigger a freeze response – if their parents are shouting over their cot they can't run away (flight) or argue with them (fight). Their only option is to stay still and hope this ensures they survive (Perry et al. 1995).

If a child has been exposed to a chronic level of stress, then their baseline state of arousal can be in a state of persistent alarm – so that even a minor event can trigger a state of alarm and a survival response. A child who spent their early years in a family where there was constant shouting and fighting can be triggered by a teacher raising their voice in the classroom to get everyone's attention and become activated into a survival response. They may appear to have switched off or disassociated in the classroom and don't respond to the teacher asking them to pay attention (freeze), they may become argumentative and refuse to co-operate (fight) or suddenly urgently need to go to the toilet (flight). Under such stress, the working of the higher parts of the brain effectively shuts down, as all the systems are focused on the need to survive. The child is not using the thinking or feeling parts of their brain; they are solely in survival mode. To help the child manage these states of alarm and to learn to regulate their own negative emotions, they need an adult who is sensitive to their distress and can calm and comfort them. The teacher who has activated the child's survival system by shouting would need to recognise what has happened and, rather than getting more irritated and cross with their apparent refusal to do as they are told, lower their voice, speak calmly to the child to acknowledge they may be feeling worried, explain that they are safe in the classroom and consider asking another adult to support them during the rest of the lesson. If the child has been triggered into rage by their sense of threat, they may throw themselves on the floor or start shouting and screaming – this is not the time to talk to them as their thinking brain has shut down. They need calming first and then there will be the opportunity to talk about what has happened. Remember when you have seen parents desperately trying to reason with a screaming toddler who wants sweets at the checkout in the supermarket? There is no talking to them at this point, as their thinking brain has switched off – once they are soothed and calmer, they might listen to their parent. To help them learn to manage these overwhelming feelings, they need the repeated experience of interaction with a calm and caring parent who can recognise and meet their needs and help them manage their feelings of rage and fear (Sunderland 2006).

Sensory integration and emotional regulation

Putting together the sound, smell, sight and feel of an event and making sense of the experience using these sensory signals is a crucial part of a child's development. It can be disrupted by the experience of early trauma. Considering the connections between your child's attachment and trauma history and their ability to process sensory signals can help make sense of how they feel and behave.

Sensory integration is the process by which the brain and the nervous system receive signals from the senses – sight, sound, smell, taste, touch, body awareness (proprioception) and movement (vestibular) – interpret these signals and act on them. For example, the sensory information that a fire is hot will be interpreted, organised and the appropriate action to move away will be signalled. The brain's ability to process these signals improves as the brain matures and is key to a child developing many areas of skill from physical skills (hand, mouth, eyes and large body movements) to cognitive (planning, memory, sequencing, organisation, attention) to emotional (happy, worried). It is also essential to a child being able to regulate their arousal (alertness) states relevant to the situation they are in. For example a different alertness state is needed when playing tennis to reading a book, sleeping or being chased by a dog. As they mature they need to be able to balance between being calm and being stimulated as well as learning how to self-calm and self-regulate (Perry *et al.* 1995; Bhreathnach 2009). In a child's very early life, they need an adult to respond to their sensory needs, as they feed, bathe, play and take care of them. The adult will balance the sensory needs of feeling hunger, thirst, cold and wet with feeling full, warm and dry. When the baby is bored, afraid or upset, the adult will meet their need and they will feel happy and safe. By the adult repeatedly identifying the baby's sensory and emotional needs and co-regulating their state of arousal to a calm state, the baby learns how to process their own sensory and emotional signals and develop effective emotional regulation and sensory integration (Radwan 2009).

But the process of developing efficient sensory integration may be impaired by certain factors such as genetic, environmental or prenatal factors, for example illness or developmental disorder. The impact of early trauma and neglect also has a detrimental impact on the child's capacity for sensory integration. With repeated exposure to high levels of stress, the child's responses may become oversensitised to stress and they are vulnerable to living in a poorly regulated state of arousal and anxiety. Rather than using the cortex to help organise an appropriate response to the signal received, only the lower parts of the brain are used and the child experiences frequent fight/flight/freeze responses and shows signs of overarousal or shutdown in response to a sensory experience. Their interpretation of and response to sensory signals is influenced by their being in a heightened state of arousal (Koomar 2009; Perry 2001; Van de Kolk 2005).

As a result of neglect, they may have had very limited opportunity for sensory experiences, and this will have impacted on their development in terms of their sensory integration. They may have spent long periods in their cot or strapped in a pushchair rather than crawling about on the floor. They may have lacked stimulation and not had opportunities to play or mix with other children. They may have been fed a very limited diet in terms of variety of texture, perhaps only eating chips or being fed only baby food and milk. They may not have had a positive attachment relationship with their carer through which they could develop their capacity to self-regulate appropriately but instead they had to develop patterns of response which allowed them to survive the neglectful or threatening parenting relationship and this has affected their capacity for sensory integration and emotional regulation.

As a result, a child may respond to everyday sensory experiences and signals differently to children who have not experienced the same difficult early history. A smell or a sound may be confusing due a lack of exposure to that sensory experience before or due to difficulty interpreting that sense at a higher level. It may also connect with a memory of a sensory experience which was painful or scary, which triggers a fear response for them. For example, a child who experienced living with alcoholic, violent parents ran and hid when her foster carer dropped a glass in front of her. A girl whose new class teacher used the same aftershave as her abusive father froze and could not answer when her teacher approached her with a question. Their sensory processing was shaped by their past experiences of trauma and triggered a survival response.

Other children may have sensory processing difficulties — they may find bright lights or harsh noise upsetting, they may hate having their teeth cleaned or their hair brushed, they may find certain T-shirts or socks uncomfortable or be fearful of being moved backwards. They may conversely seek out sensory experiences like chewing their nails or jumping and swinging. They might shrink from being touched or hug people too tightly, rush around constantly or struggle to get up and get active (Koomar 2009).

If a child struggles with regulating their sensations, this will affect their emotional state and their ability to maintain themselves at their optimum arousal level, i.e. not over- or under-responding to sensory signals but being able to come back to a calm and alert state, rather than having complete meltdowns or shutting down because they are overwhelmed. Equally, a child may struggle to regulate their emotional responses, affecting their sensory registration and responses because the sensory and emotional systems are so closely intertwined and have a significant impact on one another and on a child's arousal state.

When your child comes to live with you, they may have some difficulties with their sensory integration that you become aware of. You might want to seek professional support if you think that this is an issue for your child, for example, by asking your doctor to refer your child to an occupational therapist who can support your understanding of your child's responses to certain sensory environments and activities and the root of these. They will be able to identify which senses are challenging and how to safely go about developing the processing of those sensations as well as their emotional impact, offering home and school strategies or treatment to do this. As an adoptive parent, you can also give your child sensory-based experiences and activities that will help them to develop their sensory integration and their ability to self-regulate within the context of your developing an attachment relationship. The challenge is to begin to blend your understanding of attachment and trauma with an understanding of sensory integration to help you make sense of what your child has experienced and how it has affected them, and how this will shape your parenting of them. When you are able to identify the triggers and help them to regulate, you will over time teach them to better self-regulate. When your child is better able to self-regulate rather than being triggered into survival behaviours, they will be more able to access their thinking brain and better able to express their emotions and needs (Bhreathnach 2009; Koomar 2009).

Theoretical framework – putting the pieces together

The key ideas we need to consider to shape the introductions and early days of becoming an adoptive family are:

- The need to understand the effect of past experiences on the developing brain.

- The need to offer experiences which can develop new connections and build good bridges in the brain to improve how the brain functions and how it responds to stress.

- The need to give the child good care, which is sensitive to their needs and is relationship-based.

- The need to help the child develop secure attachment relationships, with a more positive template for the world and their relationships.

- The need to help the child grieve their losses and resolve their difficult, early experiences.

Providing good care to promote positive development and growth for children who have had a difficult early childhood is the key challenge for adopters and social workers. Hughes and Baylin's work shows the connection between offering such care and the positive impact on the child – they describe how 'brain-based parenting' helps the child's brain to grow and develop while protecting it from overexposure to stress. By parenting with PACE – playfulness, acceptance, curiosity and empathy (Hughes 2009) – the child can begin to make positive emotional relationships. If a child is given attachment-focused parenting, this will promote good connections in the brain. Rather than being triggered by poor and unsafe care into self-defence, freezing and self-reliance, the child will start to engage, trust and feel safe when they receive such attuned, attachment-based parenting (Hughes and Baylin 2012; Golding 2008).

Shaping introductions and family life based on these key ideas – by preparing to give your child a family life which is based on the principles of offering such attachment-based parenting within an attachment-friendly environment, your child will be given the opportunity to live well within a family. It will offer them the opportunity to create new templates and new memories of family life within a safe home, which recognises their early history and enables them to thrive.

CHAPTER THREE

• • • • • • • • • • •

Getting Ready

Preparing for a Child to Join your Family

Preparing for introductions

After being assessed and approved as suitable to adopt a child, you may have to wait a while until you are matched with the right child for you. How long this takes is like measuring a piece of string: it takes as long as it takes to find the right child to create your family. When you have been matched with a child, your focus shifts from looking for a child to preparing your home and your family for the arrival of your child. Some adopters start getting ready as soon as they are approved by the Adoption Panel, whereas others prefer to wait until they are matched with a child. This mirrors people preparing to have a baby – some start buying baby clothes the minute they find out about the pregnancy, whereas others wait until just before the baby arrives – this reflects your own expectations about how to prepare for a child coming to your family. All sorts of factors can influence your preparations including whether you already have a birth child or have previously adopted, how long you have waited for a child and your own expectations of the process.

When you went through the process of assessment, you will have talked about the kind of family life you are imagining with your adopted child – the meals you will cook, the way you will decorate their bedroom and the kinds of things you will do together to create a sense of family. The child you will adopt will also have ideas and wishes about the kind of family life they want to have. When they are doing preparatory work with their social worker, they often ask for pets and lots of toys and a mummy and daddy who will play with them – sometimes they wish for the impossible such as living in a palace or having eight horses and a swimming pool! Maybe you can't make all their wishes come true, but you can try to create a family life that feels safe and happy for everyone, even if you don't live in a palace!

The child you adopt will already have had the experience of living in a family – or with several different families if they have moved between foster carers or different members of their birth family. They will have had experiences that will have been frightening and left them feeling anxious and angry. These difficult early experiences will have affected their attachment relationships and their development. They will need parents who understand their need for safe parenting which acknowledges their traumatic early life history. By preparing for your child to join you while bearing in mind their need for safe parenting, as adopters you can help your child make a positive transition from their foster family to your adoptive family. Talking over preparations with your social worker can help you shape preparations to create a family environment that is sensitive to your child's attachment needs.

Preparing a book to introduce yourselves
One of the first things adopters are asked to do is prepare a book introducing themselves to their child as their new parents. You

may also be asked to make a DVD to accompany the book, to give your child a physical sense of who you are. There are all sorts of books on the market – some light up when the page turns, some use adopters' voices to tell the story and some look just like a fairy-tale storybook. While these effects can look beautiful and very professional, they can alter the focus of the book and overload the child with sound, light and colour. The book is to give your child their first look at you, their new parents – the people they will call mummy or daddy – and so the focus needs to be just on the two of you.

Keeping the book short and simple with specific pictures and few words helps your child to begin to get to know you as their new parents without feeling overwhelmed. Too much detail can leave them feeling anxious and confused. A simple book, such as a small photograph album, is good – not too heavy or difficult for small children to turn the pages of, or carry around. Laminating photographs is helpful so they are not damaged by frequent holding and touching. You can give your child several copies of the photographs so they can have them around the foster carers' home and not just in the book.

When you are adopting as a couple include photographs of you both together and as individuals – and don't forget to introduce yourselves: 'Hello, I am your new mummy, my name is ...'. The terms 'forever family/forever mummy' might be difficult for your child to understand or believe depending on their early experiences, so these are best avoided. You should also try to avoid using pictures where you are in exotic locations, wearing sunglasses, holding cocktails or pints of beer or wearing costumes, including wedding dresses and smart suits. Not being able to see people's eyes, or seeing them in unfamiliar outfits in strange locations can trigger anxiety for children – whereas choosing photos of you in clothes that you then wear to meet them for the first time can help create a sense of familiarity. Your child's experience of parties and alcohol may not have been happy experiences and seeing you engaging in similar activities may trigger difficult memories so photographs of you need to convey a sense of safety and the everyday to help promote a sense of you as safe people who can care for them and keep them safe.

When choosing photographs to put in the book, consider who and what is significant in your family and home. If you have another child, they should be in the book, but other family members can be introduced later on to avoid overwhelming the child with lots of new people. If there is someone who will be particularly significant, such as a grandparent who lives in your home or who visits daily, they should be in the book. However, including too many people dilutes the attachment relationship that you are trying to establish with your child. It may also mirror your child's own birth history, for example, if they have been moved between several different family members, this can recreate the sense of being without a specific attachment relationship. Sometimes life-story books include photographs of large gatherings of their birth family but they have little sense of the relationships between all the different people, which leads to a sense of confusion rather than one of belonging, which is the one you are trying to create with them.

If you have pets, they should also go in the book with their names and where they sleep. Some children have had very scary encounters with pets in their birth families, where dogs may have been used as guard dogs or in fights and animals may not have been looked after or trained to be safe around children. You might add a comment that your pet is friendly and likes to play with children to reassure them.

If you are going to give your child a present at your first meeting (such as a small cuddly toy) you can use this to help introduce your child to your house by taking photographs of the toy all over the house. Taking photos of the toy in their bedroom, in all the other rooms they will use and out in the garden will help develop their sense of connection and familiarity with the house they will move into. The toy will also act as a symbol of the care you will give them and the beginning of your relationship with them as their parent (Fahlberg 2012).

John and Alison were about to adopt two little boys, Steven and Jason, aged three and four. They had had several foster placements and John and Alison were anxious to make a strong connection with the boys from the first opportunity. They created an individual book for each boy, using his favourite colour for the background paper, having found this out from their current foster carers. The first photo was of the two of them introducing themselves as Daddy and Mummy, wearing the T-shirts they then wore in their DVD and to meet the boys for the first time. They had bought the boys a tiny teddy each, again in their favourite colours, and they photographed these all over the house, including in the bath and on the toilet seat, sitting in their chairs at the dining table and outside in the sandpit. They used very few words for each picture – and ended with a picture of them smiling, saying they were looking forward to being the boys' parents. They made them each a tiny key-ring book including the same pictures for the boys to carry around – and before they handed them over, they carried them around in their pockets to give them their own scent. The boys loved the books and Jason carried his around with him while Steven sat on his foster carer's lap to look at his before the day arrived to meet them. Using a multi-sensory approach and keeping the boys' developmental needs in mind helped John and Alison create a really positive first connection with the boys.

The same principles can be used when making a DVD – keep it short, simple and smiling to introduce your child to the family they will be moving in with. They may want to watch it again and again and foster carers need to be prepared to keep pressing the replay button as the visual repetition may help your child develop a sense of familiarity with the images so that they can be confortable when they meet you.

Getting the house ready

Developing a sense of connection with their new family is an important part of the process. The photographs in the introductory book will help build a picture for them of their new home. If you take photographs during introductions when you are all out together and then put these up around the house, your child will notice them on arriving and immediately has a signal that they belong in this house. Similarly, having a balance of family photographs is important. Seeing walls covered in photographs of a child already there (if you have older children) can trigger a sense of anxiety about fitting in and whether you have enough space for them as well. Be mindful of your older child's feelings too if you start moving or taking down his or her photographs. Getting them to join in to make space is a good way to help them with this process.

Displaying a photograph of your child with their foster carers can also aid the sense of connection for them. Some adopters have expressed a worry that these photographs will upset the child and stop them settling in – one adopter kept them in the bottom of the child's wardrobe rather than have them on display as she was anxious not to remind her child of her past and upset her. However, having a photo of them with their foster carers in a frame on a shelf for everyone to see can help in several ways – it can act as a prompt to talk about their foster carers and enable them to share their memories and feelings about them, as well as helping them to develop a sense of having made the move from the foster family to your family. It can also be a way to reassure them that the foster family still thinks and cares about them. When children have experienced loss and people disappearing from their lives, this can be a very important message for them to have. Some children sleep with a picture of their foster carers under their pillow for the first few weeks, or have the photo by their bed so they can see it when they wake up. They may find this comforting in the early days when everything is new and strange and they are grieving the loss of their safe and familiar foster carer.

Using these images to help them manage the separation process and reflecting on the sad and muddled feelings they may have are key roles for you in helping your child make this transition to a new family (Gray 2012b). Having this photo up on the mantelpiece and you noticing and valuing it being there signals to your child that you value this part of their lives and are happy to talk about it, rather than trying to pretend it did not exist or feeling uncomfortable about talking about their past. Your child may be sensitive to these messages as they try to work out their own story and why they moved to your family. When you are open to talking about their past history, they are less likely to feel ashamed or worry that you do not accept them because of where they have come from.

Adapting your home from a sensory perspective is another way to help your child make the transition from another family home to yours and for them to feel safe. Using the senses to create a feeling of familiarity can comfort a child in a new and strange environment, which is what their adoptive home will be to them. They may feel anxious, unsafe and stressed by moving and this may trigger memories of feeling unsafe when they were little. Helping them to feel more emotionally regulated will enable them to settle more quickly and feel safer and closer to you as their new parents. If they can be supported to feel calmer and safer in terms of their emotions, they will be better able to begin to develop positive attachment relationships and will be less easily triggered into states of alarm and fear. Creating a sensory environment which soothes them and evokes feelings and memories which are calming and familiar will help with this process (Bhreathnach 2009).

To help prepare your home, think about all the different sensations that create a sensory environment. Pay attention to how your house might smell, look and sound when compared to their foster home. Think about the tastes and textures they will encounter in your home and how you might mirror some of those from their foster home. Find out which washing powder and cleaning products the foster carers use and try using the same for a few weeks prior to your child arriving to create an environment which smells familiar. One adopter noticed that the foster carer always had a small scented candle burning on her living room window sill, so she bought the same brand and lit it on their child's first visit to their home. Using the same bubble-bath and toothpaste can also evoke a sense of familiarity, making bath-time and bedtime less stressful as they will not be surprised by unfamiliar tastes and smells. Children may bring their own sheets and pillowcases with them to help them sleep better – or you could give the foster carers pillowcases that you have slept on for the child to use, hygiene being less important than familiarity.

Finding out from foster carers about your child's favourite foods and which brands they like is helpful so that tastes are familiar and mealtimes are less stressful.

George was refusing to eat his beans on toast for dinner on the tenth day of his introductions to Sally and John. Sally felt puzzled, as she knew this was one of his favourite meals. She later checked with the foster carer when they went back to her house and she smiled: George did indeed love beans on toast, but the foster carers always bought him Heinz beans and cut the toast into little squares before piling on the beans; any other way was just not right in George's eyes. Sally tried it this way and he ate it all up – such a tiny detail, but it made all the difference to him and his ability to manage a new and strange situation.

Children may be hypervigilant to any sound or smell that may be a potential threat to them. Darkness or night-time may be particularly scary as it may trigger memories of when they were hurt or frightened. Foster carers can share what they do at night to help your child feel safe – whether they use a night light or the door left wide open. Some foster carers may not have supported children at night – whether due to following 'safe caring' guidelines for fostering or for their own reasons – and they may have made them sleep in the dark with the door firmly shut. You may want to change the routine when your child comes to live with you. Other children may struggle with being the only one upstairs if everyone else is still up and downstairs – this can trigger feelings of being abandoned all over again. Getting a little plug-in night light before they come, and showing them how it works before they go to bed on the first night, can help prepare them for their first night in a strange bedroom.

> Peter and Julie described the first night that Susan slept at their house. They bathed her and read her a story, tucked her in and turned off the light. At this she jumped out of bed and started crying, she would not settle without the main light being left on. The foster carer had not mentioned this in her description of Susan's routine. Peter and Julie decided to leave the light on even thought they could not understand how she would sleep in such bright light. Susan had heard frightening violence between her birth parents when she had been sent up to her room at night and no one had come to comfort her. Peter and Julie talked to her, reassuring her that they were there to keep her safe and they left the light on. Susan gradually developed a sense of safety with them so she no longer needed the main light on. She chose a beautiful string of pink flower night lights that they hung along the wall. Peter and Julie prioritised Susan's need to feel safe over their worry about the effect on the quality of her sleep and helped her to develop a sense that they would keep her safe.

Children may have felt scared in their bedroom; they may have been sent there as a punishment for long periods, or they may have hidden there to try to keep safe. Creating a sense of safety there is vital – bearing in mind what your child may have experienced in their bedroom, go in there, lie on the bed and listen, look around and imagine how it might feel to sleep there. Keeping the room calm and simple will help create a sense of safety – too much stuff, such as lots of posters or piles of toys, can feel overwhelming when children are trying to go to sleep.

Duvet covers with the latest cartoon heroes on them may seem child-friendly but can actually trigger anxiety. Their foster carers may report that your child loves a particular toy or cartoon, and friends' children's bedrooms may be filled with them, but given their early experiences, your child needs a calmer, safer bedroom. If you watch some of the cartoons currently on television, you may identify the very themes and feelings that you are trying to help your child recover from as the cartoon heroes battle with baddies and strange monsters, get lost and get into all sorts of trouble without safe grown-ups to help them. Your child has had a different history to your friends' children and needs a different space to sleep and play in. Calm colours and fewer triggers, lots of soft covers and blankets to cuddle up with and a night light if they are afraid of the dark, will help create the sense of safety that they need. Establishing a safe and soothing sensory environment will help your child feel settled in their new room.

You will be aware of all the things that your child did not have and missed out on when they were living in their previous home. You may want to compensate for this by giving your child lots of new things and the best of everything. However, a shiny new room with lots of new toys can be overwhelming for a child moving in.

Gary talked about his newly adopted son, Daniel. He described how he and his partner had spent a long time getting Daniel's room ready, having asked the foster carers what his favourite colours were and having put up posters of all his favourite cartoons. But since moving in, Daniel kept tearing at the wallpaper just beside his bed and spoiling it. Gary felt disappointed and puzzled as to why Daniel didn't like his new room. The social worker and Gary thought together about the information Gary had about Daniel's background. He was reminded of the extreme deprivation and neglect Daniel had suffered, living in a filthy house, with sticky floors, bare walls and a mattress on the floor with no sheets to sleep on. Moving to his new home may have triggered Daniel's memories of this earlier house. Gary realised that Daniel might have been trying to recreate a familiar environment for himself, somewhere he felt more comfortable with. Daniel may also have needed more time to feel that he deserved such a lovely room as he frequently described himself as 'a bad boy' as a way of explaining what had happened to him.

Although I am not advocating dirty rooms, be mindful of what 'newness' may trigger for your child. Mixing old in with the new may be the best way to help your child feel safe and comfortable.

A child needs space – both physically and emotionally to bring their own feelings and memories with them, as well as their toys. All of their history needs to have a place in their adoptive home – the favourite toys and happy memories as well as the battered toys and the difficult memories and feelings that they carry. Sometimes they arrive with one big heap or pile of plastic bags and adopters have commented on how much stuff there seems to be, far more than they were expecting. In the first few weeks, having those familiar toys around can help a child settle, even if the bits and pieces look scruffy and there seems to be too many of them or they should have outgrown them by now. Over time they can be slowly sorted out – some to go in the attic and some to keep in their room. Some children insist on keeping so many cuddly toys on their bed that there is barely room for them, but it may have been how they kept themselves safe and regulated sufficiently to go to sleep. Over time, you may notice that their need for so many cuddly toys in their bed may diminish as they start to use their relationship with you to keep themselves safe.

Some of the items your child brings with them may be the only things that they have left from their birth family and these possessions will be hugely significant to your child in the future. When they are older and begin to explore their past, these items will form a significant link to their history. You will be able to share the stories about their first teddy bear and the tiny outfits they wore – and show how you value these links by having looked after these things since they came to live with you.

> Sally, who adopted her daughter Jasmine when she was six, described feeling a bit overwhelmed by all the things that Jasmine had brought with her. So she created a set of boxes which, over the weeks, she and Jasmine filled with the mementos and toys she had brought with her – they did not rush but spent time talking about the things as they sorted them out. Some of the toys carried a smell of the birth home triggering anxious memories for Jasmine, which her mum was able to reflect on with her as she gave her a cuddle. Doing this together gave Jasmine the message that Sally was happy and comfortable with talking about Jasmine's past with her, and the lovely boxes reflected the value they placed on her past and her memories.

Finding out about your child

Talking with the foster carers is an invaluable way to find out more about your child and how best to prepare for their arrival. Asking questions about their routine will help you establish a similar routine in your home. This will help your child feel less anxious – a predictable routine is one of the best ways to help a child develop a sense of their world as a safe place, rather than a chaotic and unpredictable one, in which they have to struggle to keep themselves safe.

Getting foster carers to describe your child's day in lots of detail is a really useful way of finding out about their routine – starting with when they wake up right through to bedtime. Ask first about the morning routine.
On waking up:

- Do they wake up very early before the foster carers?

- Do they call out or go and find the foster carers?

- Do they sit quietly in their cot or do they play in their room on their own until called?

- Do they play with other children before coming downstairs?

- Do they have breakfast before getting ready?

- Are they hungry straightaway or less keen to have breakfast?

- Do they choose their own breakfast? Do they have a bottle first?

- Who do they eat with?

- Where do they eat?

Getting ready:

- Do they dress themselves or does the foster carer help them?

- Who chooses what they wear?

- Can they notice if it is warm or cold and choose accordingly?

- Do they brush their teeth independently or do they have supervision?

Daily routine:

- Do they have a set pattern for the day?

- Do they go out to playgroup or to the park? Do they go to nursery?

- Do people often come and visit at the house?

- Do they go shopping at the supermarket?

- Do they have other children to play with?

Play:

- How do they play?

- Do they have a favourite toy or play activity?

- Can they look after their toys?

- Do they play with other children or with adults?

- Do they play alone?

- Can they 'pretend play'? Can they take turns?

- Do they get bored easily?

- Do they like to play outside? Do they like messy play?

- Do they play safely or do they need lots of supervision?

Going out:

- If they go out, do they like going in the pushchair?

- How are they in the car?

- Do they make a fuss about being strapped in a car seat?

- Do they go to sleep in the car?

- Do they have a routine when they separate from the carer, e.g. a wave and a kiss goodbye?

- When they are reunited with the carer, do they have a hug or do they make a fuss?

Mealtimes:

- For each mealtime, what is the meal called by the foster carer?

- Do they eat well? Do they eat a variety of food or are they picky?

- Can they use a knife and fork? Do they feed themselves?

- Do they sit at the table? Do they eat with other people?

- Do they have any unusual habits such as eating too slowly or too fast?

- Do they eat too much or too little?

Bath-time:

- At bath-time, do they have a bath or a shower?

- Do they like to wash themselves or does the foster carer do it?

- How are they when having their hair washed?

- Have they been afraid of being in the bath?

- Do they protest at getting out of the bath?

Bedtime:

- Do they have a special routine?

- Do they have a story?

- Do they have a snack or a bottle?

- Do they have a special toy to tuck in with them?

- Do they have a night light or music on?

- Do they settle quickly or do they need repeated settling?

- Do they wake in the night?

- Do they have bad dreams?

- Do they call out if they need the carer?

- Do they wet the bed or get up to go to the toilet by themselves?

- Do they share a room? (adapted from Moran 2010)

The list is long but it will give you an invaluable insight into your child's life – adapt the questions to be appropriate to the child's age and development, and there may be other details that the foster carer wants to share that will be helpful. If they are looking after siblings, then adapt the questions to gain a sense of how they play and interact together.

Ask also about how the foster carer meets your child's attachment needs.

When they are upset:

- How do they know they are upset? What do they notice?

- How do they express their feelings?

- How does the foster carer soothe them?

- Are they easily soothed or does it take a long time for them to calm down?

- Do they have a special toy or cloth that they carry with them to comfort themselves?

- Do they have a dummy or suck their thumb when they are tired or upset?

When they are cross:

- What does the foster carer see when they are angry?

- Do they have tantrums?

- Do they throw or break things?

- Do they get aggressive or hurt themselves?

When they are naughty:

- What does the foster carer do?

- Do they spend time on the 'naughty step' or in time-out? Are they sent upstairs to their bedroom?

When they are hurt or sick:

- Do they seek comfort from the foster carer?

- Do they let the foster carer take care of them?

- Do they seek cuddles? (adapted from Moran 2010)

Having these conversations with their foster carers will help you shape a routine that feels familiar to your child and will give you confidence as you take over parenting them in the early days. Their answers will also help you recognise your child's attachment needs and how to meet them, as well as signalling things that your child might find hard, such as managing separations.

Preparing yourselves

You will have done lots of work during your assessment process by talking and thinking about what it will be like to be an adoptive parent. Before your child arrives you will have had time to read all about them, their history, their parents' history, the various placements they may have had and you will have gained a sense of the kind of parenting they have experienced. You will have had the opportunity to think about the impact of their experiences on their development and their attachment relationships. You will have decided that this child is the right child to join your family.

This time is also an opportunity to consider what the challenges might be in becoming this child's parent. Asking for more information if you feel there are gaps in your understanding of your child's history, and exploring in detail with your social worker how their history has affected your child's relationships and their emotional development can help prepare you to parent them in a way more attuned to their attachment needs.

Sally and Jo were about to adopt Sam and Daniel, aged two and four. As part of their preparation for the boys coming to live with them, their social worker, Jane, spent time going through all the case files for Sam and Daniel so as to put together a chronology of the boys' lives. She then made a timeline of all the moves and events that had happened from Sam's birth through to their last foster placement. As they went through the timeline together, Jane highlighted how old each boy had been at the time of each event and the impact the event might have had on their development. They counted five incidents of domestic violence during which the police had been called, and three different foster placements before the boys were one and three and then moved to their last foster home. Jane talked through with Sally and Jo how this might have affected the boys' attachment relationships as they had witnessed their parents fight and had had so many different carers. Sally and Jo were better able to understand the boys' need for safe and predictable parenting, and also acknowledged the boys' high level of anxiety as they had gained such a clear understanding of Sam and Daniel's history.

Sharing your expectations of how you will parent with your partner and social worker at this point is useful – to enable you to share your ideas of the parent you wish to become and the family life you are hoping to build. A central part of this part of preparing to be a parent is spending some time considering your own experience of being parented. In your assessment, you will have been asked to give a description of what it was like for you growing up – but there is a need to go a bit deeper than a straightforward account of your childhood. Rather than simply recalling family holidays and who was at home to look after you, exploring what your attachment relationships were like and how your emotional needs were met by your parents will help you understand your own parenting style. Thinking about what happened when you were little and needed soothing or comfort, or when something bad happened and remembering who was there to look after you, will help you understand how your own attachment pattern has developed. It may be that your own parents struggled to care for you and you have a vulnerability as a result, perhaps a tendency to avoid conflict if your parents argued a lot, or perhaps you find being on your own hard as your mother was ill a lot when you were little and you felt anxious about where she was and who would look after you.

Kim Golding emphasises in her book *Nurturing Attachments* (2008) that a perfect childhood is not essential, and difficult early childhood experiences do not prevent anyone from parenting. But to be able to develop a secure style of parenting and build secure attachments with a child, you as the adult need to be able to make sense of your childhood and have resolved any difficulties. If you as the adult have a secure attachment pattern, your child is more likely to develop the same secure pattern.

If you find that there are things in your own childhood that you are still struggling with or find hard to think or talk about when exploring your own account of your past, seeking some support to make sense of these childhood experiences can be helpful and enable you to become the parent that you want to be (Golding 2008; Siegel and Hartzell 2004).

CHAPTER FOUR

● ● ● ● ● ● ● ● ● ● ● ●

Preparing Family
and Friends

Part of getting ready involves the rest of the family and the people close to you. Preparing to welcome a new member of their extended family is a really exciting process for grandparents, aunts, uncles and cousins. But unlike when a new baby arrives, the child that comes by adoption already has a history and experiences that will impact on their joining an extended family. They will have already experienced the loss of their birth parents and will have lived with other carers. They may also have experienced hurt and neglect when living with their birth family – so even if they are very young when they join your family, they will carry these experiences with them and will need particular support and parenting to enable them to thrive and build positive attachment relationships within their new family (Verrier 1993).

Some preparatory work with everyone, which acknowledges this difference, can help this new arrival to be a more successful and positive experience for the family. As adopters, you will need the support of your family and friends and if they are well prepared and informed, they will be better able to give you that support.

Preparing your older children

If you already have children, spending time thinking about adoption and what it means is a good place to start. Give them a simple explanation that some children cannot live with the parents they were born to and need to live with another family. Depending on their age, your children might need more details and may even have some tricky questions for you to answer about why you are not having another baby or why another mother would give their baby away. Help them to think about what good parents do and why some parents find this hard to do. You could make a list with them of all the things mums and dads do to look after their children – top of the list is usually playing with and feeding them, followed by keeping them warm, clean and safe, taking them to the doctor and loving them. You can use your list to help your children understand that some people find it hard to do these things for their children so the children need to go and live with another family who know how to do such things. They will also need to learn that children who are going to be adopted will live in a foster family for a while and foster carers are people who look after children in their family while the social worker looks for the right family. Introduce your social worker to them as someone whose job it is to find families for children who cannot live with their birth family. Read them stories about adoption or try using Heidi Argent's book about adopting a brother or sister to help prepare them and give them the opportunity to ask the questions that may be worrying them (Argent 2010). Drawing and thinking together about why children are adopted and helping them to think about what it might be like to have an adopted brother or sister can help prepare them (Macliver and Thom 1990).

Sharing their worries

As with birth children, the arrival of a new sibling creates anxiety; as a parent, being open and sensitive about this with your children can help them deal with their feelings about the new arrival and the changes this will bring. Involving your children already in the family in getting the photographs and book ready is a positive way to engage them in the process of preparing for a sibling to join them in their family. It offers the opportunity to talk about some of the things they may want to show the child – their pets, bedroom, favourite places to play in the garden – as they help you take pictures of all these things for the book. They can share some of their hopes and expectations about what it would be like to have a brother or sister – having someone new to play with and someone to go on trips with and have fun with. It also gives them time to share some of the worries they may have about another child coming to live with them – the 'what ifs' that they may be worrying about. What if they break their toys? What will happen if they are naughty? What if they fight? What if they don't like each other?

Getting the book ready together can offer a great opportunity to start exploring some of their own feelings about a new child coming to live with their family while they are focused on the task of choosing and sticking things in the book with you. Adopted children may want to look at the book you made for them when they came, and just as birth children may ask to hear the story of when they were born, they may want to hear the story again of when they first came to live with you.

As a parent, you will have talked about these things with your children during the assessment process, and your social worker will also have spent some time exploring these worries with them – but with the imminent arrival of another child, children may experience strong feelings of worry and anxiety which they need time and support to work through. Cohen, in his book

Playful Parenting, talks about the fundamental questions raised by having a sibling – when another child arrives, the child will wonder whether they are still really wanted and whether their parents will stop loving them if they start to love the new child (Cohen 2001). If they do not articulate these questions, they may communicate them through changes in their behaviour; they may become more clingy, less likely to do as they are told or become more argumentative.

Cohen uses the image of each child having an empty cup, which they learn will be filled by their parents with love to meet their needs – and that they need to learn that there is enough to fill and keep filling each cup, no matter how many children they have. Children need reassurance that their worries are heard and that there is enough love for everyone (Cohen 2001).

If children have experienced parenting which involved their cups not being filled consistently with love and care or did not have their needs met, they may struggle to believe this and may perceive another child coming as a threat to their well-being and survival. In their experience of the world, they need to make sure that their cup is filled or they will not survive – sharing is not an option for them. They need much more reassurance that their need for love and care will be met even when their parents are also looking after another child.

Sharing their story

When a child with a history of traumatic experiences joins a family, the siblings will need careful preparation so they have the best chance of joining together as a new family. Older siblings will need a story that helps them understand why this child is coming to live with them – perhaps by linking it to their own story if they have also been adopted or by talking to them about why some children can't live with the parents they were born to. They don't need lots of details as this can be scary and overwhelming, but they do need a true sense of why this child is joining your family. The sibling will also need some time to work out with you what to do if something goes wrong and one of their worries becomes real. They may also need some support to manage the onslaught of curiosity from their friends and people at school to explain why they have a new brother or sister.

Joseph, aged eight, announced at teatime that he did not want his mum to come and pick him up from school anymore once his new sister Kelly had arrived. He then got down from the table and said he was ready to go to his swimming lesson. In the car, his mum asked him why he did not want her to come and collect him, telling him she liked to come and meet him and that he was too young to walk home on his own. Joseph became upset and eventually managed to tell his mum that he was really worried all the other kids would keep asking him where Kelly had come from, as his mum wasn't fat like Tom's mum who was due to have a baby about the same time as Kelly was due to move in. After a hug and a hot chocolate at the pool, they agreed that she would talk to his class teacher and she would help him with his story. Joseph's mum phoned his teacher the next day and she agreed to help. Over the next few weeks, his teacher gave some lessons about different kinds of families and how there were lots of ways of becoming a family – as part of this, the children did a project about their own family and then shared these with their classmates so they learnt about adoption along with thinking about families with step-children, families with one parent or two and families with two mums or two dads. When the day came for Joseph's mum to bring Kelly to the playground, he was ready to introduce her to his friends.

One adopter recalled that in her family, the older children needed lots of reassurance that having a little brother would not disrupt their lives – that they could still go to dance and to football and that they wouldn't have to babysit all the time. Setting clear boundaries will help – Gray suggests letting older children know it is all right to keep their bedrooms as their private space, that they won't have to play with the little one all the time but can have time to play with their own friends and do their homework (Gray 2012a).

If it is possible that a child may present sexualised or aggressive behaviour when they join your family, there needs to be a discussion about this with your social worker to help you plan how to keep everyone safe. Give your children a clear message that there will be no secrets in the family and that if they are worried or something happens, they need to tell a grown-up. You can all work out together in advance which grown-ups they can talk to, so they are clear that they can talk to you when they are at home, or to a particular teacher who knows their family situation if they need to talk to someone at school.

Helping older children in your family understand that other children may not have had the same loving and caring experiences that they have had can be a challenge – keeping your new child's story confidential while helping the other children to understand why they are coming to live with you is a delicate balance for parents. You may feel you want to protect your children from the idea that, in some families, children aren't cared for and bad things happen and perhaps they are too young to be exposed to such sad ideas. Introduce the idea in a low-key way, without too much detail at first. Using storybooks and television programmes can be a good way of starting these conversations about the different kinds of family experiences children may have. What you choose to share about the child's story needs to be pitched at an appropriate developmental level. As the children grow and ask more questions in the future, you can develop the complexity of the story and give them more detailed explanations.

Issues for adopted children

If you have already adopted a child, the arrival of another adopted child can trigger issues for them that need particular consideration. It may reawaken feelings of loss and anxiety that they have not felt since their own early months in your family.

It may trigger memories of living in their birth family when you start to talk about why this child is coming to live with your family and why they can't live with their birth parents. Starting the process of introductions and meeting foster carers can remind them of their own time spent living with foster carers and they may be curious about what their foster carers are doing now and who they are looking after, especially if you have not kept in touch with them since the child moved to live with you. Travelling to meet a new brother or sister and the sense of disruption to their lives can evoke a strong sense of anxiety. Seeing suitcases and bags, moving rooms around and other people coming to look after them while you are at meetings can all trigger a sense of unease that their world is changing. Keeping their routine the same as much as is possible, so they still go to football practice and to friends for tea while introductions are happening, can help maintain a sense that their world is staying predictable and safe. When you are asked to do bath-time and bedtime routines at the foster carers' home with your new child, thought needs to be given as to who will put your older child to bed. They may be old enough to stay up and wait for you, or you and your partner may decide to take it in turns. This needs talking over in the planning stages so everyone can acknowledge your need to balance the needs of both children otherwise you can end up feeling torn between them and worrying about the child you have left at home. The same applies to the school-run – the challenge is to manage the needs of both children during the intense period of introductions so neither feels abandoned by you.

Depending on their age, this may lead them to ask questions about their own adoption and they may need time with you to explore their questions and memories. Getting their life-story books out and looking at their family photographs and retelling their own adoption story can help them to make sense of the feelings roused by a new brother or sister joining them through adoption.

If you have older adopted children, another child joining the family can trigger anxiety in them about their current place in the family – as one adoptive boy said: 'Perhaps they just want to replace me.' Given their experience of leaving one family to join another, they may feel replaceable and will therefore have to move again. They may not trust the idea that they will be with you until they grow up; they may also feel that they are not good enough and that is why you want another child to be in your family. Your delight in having another child may also confirm that they are just not good enough. You may notice changes in how they behave; they may struggle with schoolwork or with managing things they can usually do. They may behave as they did when they first came to live with you, talking and playing like a younger child and seeking much more attention from you. They may try extra hard to be especially good or start being very awkward and difficult. All these behaviours signal to you that they are struggling with the implications of having a new adopted brother or sister.

Notice these changes and reflect on their worries as you prepare for the new arrival. Enabling your children to feel safe and cared for in the face of such a big change in their family can present you with unexpected challenges. Try to take an approach that encompasses reflective parenting. Stay empathic and curious about how your children are experiencing this change and reflect with them about how it feels for them to have an adopted little brother or sister. Taking this approach can help your children to feel safe and understood as they come to terms with the change and what it means for them. For example, you could wonder out loud whether your son or daughter might be worrying that mum and dad will not have time for them anymore or might like their new child better than them. Before you rush to reassure them that you will love them both the same, accept that they may feel differently and it may take time for them to trust that you will love them just as much as your newly adopted children. Or you might ask whether thinking about what their new brother or sister has been through reminds them of the scary things that happened to them before they came to live with you. You can acknowledge how hard this might be for them and reassure them that you are there to keep them safe and help them not to feel afraid. Starting those conversations can help your first adopted child to feel that you accept that they may have difficult feelings about having a new sister or brother, and that you want to understand them and support them (Golding and Hughes 2012).

Preparing family members

Other members of your family may also need support in thinking about the child who will join your extended family. Parents who have longed to be grandparents may have all sorts of ideas about what they are going to do with their new grandchild – they may have plans for trips out and tea at their house, maybe having them to stay over. They may already have grandchildren and be looking forward to seeing them all playing together, joining in family parties and celebrations. Prospective aunts, uncles and cousins will also have plans and ideas to welcome the new member of the family. For this to be successful, you may want to call a family meeting to talk about how best they can support you in the early weeks and to discuss what the possible difficulties might be and how you want to deal with these. Using this time to give family and friends some information about attachment and trauma can help prepare them to support you – giving them stories about adoption and some books on attachment and trauma to read can help develop their understanding of the challenges you may face, and explain why you want to parent in a way which may appear different from their own way of doing things.

Sharing your child's story

One of the first things to consider is the child's story and how much of this you want to share with your family – you need to balance the child's right to have their story kept private with the need to share some of their history to explain their coming to live with you. Some adopters decide not to share any information, believing that their child can tell their story when they feel ready to share it and that it is not their right to share the story first.

They might give a very simple explanation that the child could not be looked after by their birth family. As adopters, you may be asked lots of questions as family members and friends want to know more. If you have always shared things in the past, they may find it strange that you suddenly do not want to tell them everything. They may not have considered that you do not want to answer these questions and may feel hurt that you are shutting them out. Even people you hardly know can be astoundingly nosey about your new family – stopping you in the playground or in the middle of the supermarket to ask about your new child and where they came from. This can take you by surprise and you may say more than you intended. Spending time to prepare with your social worker for these conversations can help you decide how you are going to respond and the story you will share when asked.

Cousins may also need preparation, using stories and play, to understand that some children can't live with their birth families and need another mummy and daddy to look after them. Without an explanation, they may repeatedly ask questions which may make the adopted child feel uncomfortable and leave them all feeling anxious, rather than accepting each other as new parts of the family.

Alison and John recently adopted Julie as a younger sister for David, who was also adopted, and they all went to a big family wedding. All the children were outside in the garden playing. When John wandered out to see how they were getting on, he spotted David looking hot and bothered surrounded by several of his cousins. As he walked over he overheard David saying, 'just shut up, just shut up, I've told you OK, she just *is* adopted!' After calming David down, John decided to ask his brother and sister over to talk about what had happened. He offered to lend them some storybooks about adoption to read with their own children to teach them about adoption and to support Julie and David in becoming part of the extended family. He suggested that if they had any questions, they should ask him or Alison. David needed reassurance that he didn't have to answer their questions and that he could get an adult to help him when he got stuck with a situation he was struggling to deal with.

Thinking about attachment and trauma

Spending time thinking about the impact on children of the experiences they have had – without going into the exact personal details of your child – can be really helpful in preparing the extended family. Developing their knowledge of attachment and trauma, perhaps with the help of your social worker, can deepen their understanding of your adopted child's needs and possible issues. Asking your family to read stories about children who have experienced early life trauma can be a good way to introduce them to these ideas and there are books written specifically for people who are becoming adoptive grandparents and family to help them prepare themselves.

To begin creating secure attachment relationships with a child who has experienced fear, loss and change, you as parents should focus on creating a sense of safety for your child. You will parent them in a way which enables them to feel they can trust you as safe adults who will care for them and not hurt or frighten them (Golding and Hughes 2012). This can sometimes appear quite different from the parenting that your grandparents, aunts and uncles have given to their own children who have not had the same frightening experiences and do not need such a focus on safety. What they observe you doing as new adoptive parents may not reflect their own model and style of parenting. This can lead to misunderstandings and unintended criticism which may leave you feeling hurt. Your family may question why you aren't sending the child to their room when they have been naughty or why you are not having a big welcome party for your child. They can feel disappointed that they are not allowed to take the child out with them in the early days and they may express concern that you as new parents aren't setting strict enough boundaries and may be being badly treated by your new child. Friends with children of the same age may wonder why you are not inviting them over for play-dates straightaway – or they may feel slightly aggrieved that you do not follow the advice they offer you. Helping them to develop an understanding of why you are parenting in a different way, and how this looks in practice, can prevent family and friends from feeling puzzled, helpless and excluded. Being open about some of the issues, while clear about the way you want to parent, can help them to support you when you need it most and avoid misunderstandings.

Sally had adopted May and Emma and introduced them to their new grandparents two weeks after the girls' arrival – everything had been going well and the girls were excited to meet Granddad and Granny. The grandparents arrived with a small present for each girl – May said 'thank you' with a big smile and promptly sat on her granny's lap, Emma hid behind her mum and refused to open her present. They decided to go out for a walk to the park. Despite Sally telling May to hold her hand, May refused and insisted on walking with Granny. Emma cried and begged Sally to pick her up – her granddad told her she was quite big enough to walk and far too heavy for her mum to carry. By the end of the visit, Sally described feeling exhausted – she was worried that the girls had seemed rude; Emma hadn't said 'thank you' or talked much at all and May had refused to do as she was told. Neither grandparent had seemed to recognise that the girls were struggling with their first visit and they seemed disappointed with the grandchildren they had waited so long to meet. Talking about how the girls' attachment behaviours had been triggered by meeting these new people – May trying to please and letting a stranger look after her, whereas Emma became clingy and withdrawn – helped the grandparents understand the impact of the girls' early experience on their behaviour. It also helped them to consider their daughter's worries about what they might think and their expectations of the girls. They had always encouraged their children to be polite and independent so they were troubled by their daughter agreeing to carry her little girl and the lack of a thank you. They were able to recognise how they measured their daughter's parenting and their granddaughters' responses against their own parenting style.

Nicky described feeling quite put out by her newly adopted son James's positive response to his grandparents in the early days – when he was thirsty he asked them for a drink and when he bumped his knee he ran to his grandma for a cuddle. His grandparents were only too happy to scoop him up for cuddles and loved feeding him his favourite chocolate buttons and wiping his nose when he had been crying. Nicky was left feeling rejected and hurt – despite her best efforts, James seemed to prefer his grandparents. Talking this over, they were able to see how their eagerness to become his grandparents stopped them from understanding that he needed to develop his relationship with his mother. His survival strategy to get anyone to look after him connected with their instinctive desire to care for him. But he needed to develop a secure attachment relationship with one specific person to get his needs met. They recognised that, on future visits, if they returned him to his mum when he needed something, this would help build this relationship. If he was hungry or had hurt himself, they needed to take him to Nicky so she could give him the care and nurture he needed and he would then learn that he could depend on her to look after him.

Social workers can experience the same issue when visiting – a cute baby is just asking to be picked up, and a toddler offering kisses is hard to resist. But children in a new adoptive home need to learn that they do have an adult who will meet their need for a cuddle or affection and they do not need to seek it from a stranger. Social workers should gently direct children to their parents for cuddles and kisses rather than giving them themselves.

Support network meetings

In the early weeks when children are getting to know you as their parent, your network of family and friends can play a positive role in supporting you as a family. Talking about how you plan to parent and how this might appear different to their expectations can help them support you – with an emphasis on your primary role to become the person who provides a sense of safety for your child. Acknowledging that this might feel difficult, and that everyone will have high expectations and experience some disappointment and worry as the process starts, might help it go more smoothly.

Sometimes agencies will arrange a series of network meetings to help this process go smoothly. You will be asked to identify who you want to invite to the meetings – usually most of the extended family who will be involved, as well as close friends who will be part of your support network. The network meeting is organised and chaired by a social worker, usually the link worker for your family. The first meeting starts by identifying how everyone is linked to you. Information is then given about the impact of early trauma on children and their need for a different type of parenting. Some of the difficulties that children may have in the early days when they are grieving the loss of their foster carers while dealing with the stress of moving to live with a new family are highlighted. There will be a discussion about the need for your child to be parented in relation to their developmental age rather than their chronological age, given their past experiences. What that looks like in practice is shared using examples to help everyone gain a better understanding of parenting children who have experienced early trauma. Your family are encouraged to plan how to prepare children who are already in the extended family to welcome a child with a different early history to their own. Further discussion focuses on how your extended family and close friends can offer support – from practical ideas such as helping with the laundry or doing the shopping, to committing to offering telephone support in the evenings or taking the older children out. There may be a further network meeting when the introductions are imminent to consider the particular needs of the child that you are matched with and to share their story in so far as it is appropriate. Your extended family and friends have the opportunity to ask any questions and to voice any worries. Details of the support being offered are also organised at this meeting so everyone is clear about his or her role in the process.

When your network is well informed about the needs of the child joining your family, and understands the behaviour they may see and how you aim to support your child, you will feel less undermined or criticised and better supported. If the support is clear and sustained, you will feel less isolated and overwhelmed if things become difficult. You will be better able to meet the challenges of parenting a child who has experienced trauma, as your network will not fall away through misunderstandings. When approaching introductions, some of this groundwork can be done before you have any set dates for moving in – the more prepared you all are, the better the process will feel.

CHAPTER FIVE

● ● ● ● ● ● ● ● ● ● ●

Preparing Children to Move

Before your child comes to live with you, they need help preparing for the move. They need to make sense of their past, say their goodbyes and to look forward to joining your family. They will need to understand their story – from what happened when they were living with their birth parents to coming into care, and then the plans for their future as your adopted child. The preparation they receive will be shaped by their age and developmental level, with older children needing more detail and more active work to prepare them for the move. Your role is to understand their story and how they have been prepared for their move to join your family – once they are living with you, your role will be to carry on adding to their life-story and to create the next chapters with them.

Life-story book

The social worker will put together a life-story book which you will be given when your child moves in with you. This book will have photographs and information about your child's history which you will use as your child grows up and needs to understand their past. The book will include pictures of the birth family, where they were born and all the places that they have lived, as well as pictures of foster carers and other people who were significant to them. It will also tell their story up until they move in with you. Take time to look through the book and become familiar with it before you share it with your child, although if they are older they may have been actively involved in putting it together and already know what's in it. Reading it together, or simply looking at all the pictures together, gives you the opportunity to demonstrate that you know all of their story and are not going to reject them or think less of them because of it. Sometimes the book may be incomplete or late arriving – it needs to be an accurate reflection of your child's story and will occasionally need further work. Read it and if you feel that it needs more work, discuss this with your social worker, as it is important that this story is an accurate reflection of your child's history.

The book may be lacking information – such as not giving details about a birth father, and the social worker might ask the child to draw a picture of what they think they might look like. The story needs to be honest and accurate – it needs to be an authentic story rather than a 'fluffy' version. The story is an account of the child's lived experience and needs to acknowledge the difficult things that happened rather than gloss over them. Using social work jargon such as 'neglect and physical abuse' to describe why a child came into care is unhelpful and meaningless to a child. Giving concrete examples to explain what happened will be more helpful in aiding a child to understand their story. Writing 'Ellie's mum found it hard to remember when to give her a bottle and when to change her, and sometimes she got angry and shouted at Ellie', will give enough detail for your child to make sense of their experience, rather than saying 'Ellie suffered neglect and emotional abuse'. The details about birth parents' histories and social-services meetings and actions can be kept for the 'Letter for Later Life' that the social worker will also write and give to you for your child to read when they are older and need to have more information about the reasons they were adopted.

The story will explain why your child came into care in an age-appropriate way. Key messages it needs to include are why the birth parents did not look after your child and that it was not the child's fault they were in care: the responsibility for what happened lay with the adults who were supposed to be looking after them. There will be a whole range of reasons why – but starting with the idea that their birth parents could not manage to look after them creates the foundation for exploring their story. Young children need only a very simple explanation – that their mummy and daddy could not look after them properly, even when they were being given help, and they could not stay with parents who were not looking after them or were hurting them. As your child grows older, they will need more details about what happened in their story. Sometimes social workers create books with several different sections – one for when the child is young and then other more detailed sections for when they are older. When a story contains particularly sensitive information, such as that the child has been sexually abused, the social worker may make a separate book with this information in it to be kept separately. Children often want to show their books to visitors, including the milkman, or take the book into school for 'show and tell' day, but some of their information needs to stay private. Think about where you are going to keep the book when it is given to you – it needs to be safe so that it won't get damaged but accessible so your child can look at it when they need to. One adopter had put her daughter's book up on the top of her wardrobe as she didn't want her to read all the information too early – then one day when she was busy her daughter climbed up, took it down and then read her story by herself. If you feel your child is not ready for all the information then separate the parts you want to save until they are old enough or curious enough to want to read them, and make the rest available for them to read as and when they want to. In the early days of placement, some children want to look at their book over and over again, as a way of making sense of their move, whereas others show no interest at all. If you are interested and available to look at it with them, you can give them the message that you know and accept their story, including any difficult and shaming parts, and still want to be their parent.

Max, aged four, had moved to live with his adoptive mum and dad. His book had several chapters as he had a difficult story to tell. His adopters, Julie and Keith, were worried about how to talk to him about why he had come to live with them. The first chapter had photographs of him with his birth mother and father, of him with his foster carers, of his previous adopters, then photos of his foster carers again before ending with photos of him with Julie and Keith. It explained that his tummy mummy and daddy could not care for him so he had moved to live with his foster carers. He had then moved to live with another adoptive family for a little while but they could not care for him properly so he moved back to his foster carers. Then he had moved to live with Julie and Keith where he was going to live until he was a grown-up. The following chapter added more photographs, including all the houses he had lived in as well as the hospital he had stayed in and a map of all his moves. The story continued to add more detail about how his tummy mummy and daddy had drunk too much wine so they could not look after him. It also told the story of his first adoptive family where the parents had started fighting and he had been hurt so he had stayed in hospital for a while. The last chapter gave more details about his birth mother's and father's struggles and their involvement with social services. It also gave more details about the breakdown of his first adopters' relationship and the injuries to Max. Julie and Keith used this story to help them explain Max's history to him as he grew up and asked more questions about what had happened – their first instinct had been not to talk about what had happened and not to tell him about his first adoptive family. But with support, they were able to recognise the importance of sharing all of his story with him, as it was Max's lived experience.

The life-story book will be a valuable resource for you and your child as they grow up and need to explore who they are. As their parent, you can join with them in making the next chapters of the book. Take lots of photographs during introductions and keep souvenirs of the places you visit in the early days so you can create the next chapter. Adding a new family tree and the photographs of the adoption day celebrations, your first meal out together and their first day at their new school will become part of their history in your family. It will help create a coherent story for them.

Life-story work

Alongside the book about their life, doing work about their life history will help children process and resolve their feelings about what has happened to them. Often children have a jumble of images and memories which they struggle to make sense of – they cannot put the fragments they remember into any sense of order or make meaning from them.

Ben, aged seven, had come into care at four – his birth mother had fled his birth father who was violent and addicted to drugs. Ben and his mother had moved between hostels and a refuge in their town before returning to live with his father. After being removed by the police, Ben stayed with an emergency foster carer for two weeks before moving to another foster home. This placement was not successful and Ben moved again. When his adoptive mother drove him to school, he would see places where he thought he had stayed and would become upset but they seemed to be different places each time. Ben was struggling to create a coherent story from the memories these places triggered.

Life-story work puts past experiences into context and gives the child a chronology so they can develop an understanding of their history. It also helps them to develop a sense of the order of events in their lives. It gives them a story to make sense of why they are in care and why they are moving to a new family. A child who does not have this clear story can be confused about why they are moving to a new family – they can create fantasies about what happened in their birth families rather than understand and accept the reality. Some children simply do not know the truth – they have been afraid to ask or have not had anyone that they could ask. They may make up their own explanations for why they are in care or are being adopted. Some children pinpoint one incident or one comment they have overheard and build their explanation around that.

> Billy, aged five, told his social worker that the police had put him in foster care because he had run away – something his birth mother had told him in a contact visit. In reality, he had been found aged two by the police. He was wandering on the street looking for food late at night as his mother had had a party and left the front door open.

> Jemima, aged six, told her social worker that she had heard her birth mother (who had mental health issues) tell her foster carer that 'the kids were too much for her' and Jemima felt she and her brothers had made her mum ill because they were too naughty.

> Sally, aged seven, who had been placed as a baby with her adopters, was looking at her life-story photographs with her adoptive mum and asked her why she had bought her and not another baby.

Often children struggle to make sense of what has happened to them or why the very grown-ups who should have loved and cared for them have hurt them and did not look after them. Being told that their parents loved them, when they have memories of being hit, hurt and left hungry, does not make sense. Often, the only way they can make sense of this is to blame themselves – thinking it must be because of what they did or because they are bad that their parents behaved towards them as they did. They may feel vulnerable and have a deep sense of shame in sharing this. In helping them start to alter their perception of themselves and develop a more positive sense of their identity, life-story work plays a crucial role.

The life-story work needs to be planned carefully so it is tailored to the child's emotional and developmental level. Very young children don't have the language or cognitive ability to understand 'adoption' and 'foster care' as concepts, but using these words in preparatory work creates the foundation for building their understanding as they get older and you carry on the work with them. The work needs enough time so they are not rushed or overwhelmed by the information and their emotions. The work offers them the opportunity to resolve difficult feelings about their past experiences. To facilitate this, it is best if your child undertakes the work with their current attachment figure. Inviting their foster carer to be part of the preparatory work ensures that the child is supported by their key attachment figure as they engage in the work. The foster carer may need additional support to help them to participate in the work so they can cope with its emotional intensity and feel enabled to support the child.

Sometimes there isn't the optimum time available – the social worker might fall sick or the foster carer might have family issues that mean the preparatory work needs to be hurried along. An unfamiliar social worker might step in and do their best in the time available – if this has been the case for your child, they may need further work once they have moved.

Alex was three when her foster carer fell ill, just as she had been matched with her adoptive parents. Everyone agreed that rather than move her to another interim placement, they would all work intensely to prepare Alex to move. Her social worker used laminated photographs of the foster family and the adoptive family to introduce the idea of moving from one family to another to Alex as part of her own story (she had never lived with her birth mother as she had come straight from hospital to her foster carer). She brought a story of a duck that has to go and live with another family of ducks for her, and Alex read it every day with her foster carer. They used sets of toys ducks to play out the story in and out of the bath. They played houses with a tiny toy suitcase and made up Alex's own story about moving which the social worker gave to the adopters to keep on using when Alex moved to live with them. This was an intense period of work, but using toys and stories appropriate to her young age gave Alex a sense of her own story and enabled her to participate in the work.

The life-story work will consider the child's identity and history – they need a sense of who is who in their life and what happened. Joy Rees' model of life-story work advocates starting in the middle, i.e. in the present, before moving backwards to consider the past or forward to think about the future. This model acknowledges the child's need to feel safe, secure and grounded in the present before moving to consider things which are more scary and difficult to think about or remember (Rees 2009).

Life-story work should start with thinking about your child's life in the present. Activities might include:

- drawing the house they live in now

- making a family tree for the family they live with now

- using booklets like 'All about me' (Bruzzone 2013) to explore what they like and don't like, their hobbies and favourite activities

- taking photographs of 'now', about their current family life

- drawing their portrait and body outline, exploring what they look like

- playing sensory and attachment-based games to build their trust and connection such as hand and face painting and hide-and-seek.

Once they have explored their identity and place in the present, the social worker and their foster carer will support them to move to explore their past history using a range of approaches, which match the child's developmental level. These will include:

- putting together a collection of photographs of all the people and places that are relevant

- writing together a simple story about what happened and giving an explanation of why they are in care

- playing with puppets to enact their story or using a story the social worker has written which reflects their own experience

- reading stories together about being lost and found, being in trouble and being helped, coming into care and being adopted

- playing games about moving and joining families such as playing with ducks or dolls as families, looking after baby dolls, trains and cars on journeys, dolls and a doll's house to explore who lives with whom

- playing games which symbolise moving and permanency – hide-and-seek, rolling balls, marbles and racing cars.

The direct work may start with thinking about families, asking children to identify what children need and what parents do to look after their children. Often children focus on the very practical tasks such as cooking the tea or washing their clothes and they may need prompting to think about emotional tasks such as taking care of them when they are sick, or giving them a hug when they are sad. Exploring different kinds of families at this stage is useful – asking them to draw all the different kinds of families they can think of; with one parent or two, with two mums or two dads or one dad, one mum, with step-parents or grandparents.

Identifying the different parents they have and will have is next – they need to understand that their tummy mummy or birth mummy is the parent in whose tummy they grew in before they were born, that their birth daddy is the parent, who put the seed in their mummy's tummy to help them to grow, that their foster daddy and/or mummy are the parents who look after them, as their birth parents are not able to, and that their adoptive mummy and/or daddy are the parents who will look after them until they are grown-up and have their own family.

By using drawing and pictures, they can start to identify what they would have needed when they were at home with their birth family. The work then moves on to consider what their birth parents struggled with in trying to look after them – for very little children, this is kept to a simple explanation that they did not know how to do all the things that children need to grow up safe and well. With older children, it can explore in more detail how their birth parents struggled. They might need explanations of the issues their birth parents had difficulties with using language that is child-friendly. Some common issues that need explanation include:

- Depression – mum was feeling very sad and tired, she often lay on the sofa and forgot to make the tea.

- Domestic violence – dad hit mum, he was unkind to her, he broke the law and the police came, everyone was scared and it is not OK to hit or hurt anyone.

- Neglect – mum and dad did not have any money, they did not know how to be parents, they did not buy food or cook the tea, and they did not keep the house clean or give their child a bath or clean clothes.

- Alcohol/drug addiction – dad and mum drank a lot of beer, sometimes it made them feel good so they drank some more, but then it made them grumpy and they did not keep their children safe or feed them as they spent their money on more beer.

- Suicide – dad was feeling very sad, lots of people tried to help him feel better, but he did not stop feeling sad and he decided that he did not want to live, everyone felt very sad and missed him.

With some issues, there might be details that are too difficult to include but they could be recorded somewhere to share when the child is old enough and the social worker might explain that when they are older they can hear more of their story. With each story, the key is to emphasise that it was not the child's fault and they were not responsible for what went wrong (NLAFC 2013).

The story might include the statement that their birth parents loved them but could not look after them – this comment might try to soften the knowledge that their birth parents hurt and neglected them but it can lead to confusion about the meaning of this 'love'. Saying that their birth mother 'loved them, but …' needs exploring with them. The story could say that their birth parents gave them life, that their birth mother gave birth to them and therefore their birth parents loved them. But they did not keep them safe or look after them, they needed parents who could love them and care for them as little children need; to love them as a mummy and daddy not just as a birth parent (Foxon 2001).

The work will help the child develop an understanding of their story that is emotionally honest and developmentally appropriate – it needs to reflect their actual experience and acknowledge the complexity of emotions that the story carries for them. Activities that they might use include:

- drawing out their story on large pieces of paper (wallpaper is good)

- mapping out where people have lived, moves, events with dates

- using pictures and symbols to tell the story – maybe using a subject the child is interested in – a train-track, a road or river, with trains, cars, boats to tell the story with rocks, bridges, tunnels, storms, fires and crashes to symbolise events along the journey

- using colours and symbols to add the emotions connected with the story – chalks and pastels to shade in different emotions over different times, sun, rain, lightening to highlight different feelings.

Using these different approaches to telling the story enables the child to express and resolve feelings evoked by their experiences and share them in the work.

Danny, aged seven, had moved many times with his sisters and birth mother. She had mental-health issues and kept moving to feel safe. She went into hospital when Danny was five and he was separated from his sisters. He stayed with three different foster families before his social worker started to talk about finding him an adoptive family.

As part of the preparation for him to move, his social worker and foster carer started some life-story sessions with Danny. He was a good drawer and loved trains so they began to map out his story in tracks and stations. He drew himself as a little engine, with separate trains for his birth mother and sisters who all went down separate tracks. He drew a landslide across the tracks for the time when his mother went into hospital and used red flags to show his angry feelings about what had happened to him on his journey so far, having had to stop at so many different stations. His foster carer sat and held the pens, sitting close by him to help him with the feelings his story evoked. His social worker added in the dates to help put all the moves in order for him and drew little signals pointing out the direction his train was moving in. She drew a station controller who directed the trains and added the explanations about his separation from his mother and sisters. During his introductions to his adopters, Danny and his social worker showed them his drawing and talked about his story – they promised to keep the drawing safe and to help him add to it once he had moved to live with them at their house which would be his 'safe station'.

Sometimes there are gaps in the story and these need to be acknowledged to help make sense of their story – otherwise your child might make up their own fantasy to fill in the missing information.

Millie, aged six, was helping to put her life-story book together. She had a photo of herself with her birth mother in hospital but no photo of her father. Her social worker asked her to draw one to fill in the page and wondered what she thought he might look like. Millie drew a picture of a very scary face, with lots of teeth in a huge mouth, round red eyes and big hands. In her next session, Millie saw her drawing and asked to draw another picture – this time the face looked cheerful with blue eyes and a smile and she asked to stick this over the other picture in her book. Her foster carer was curious about this and Millie was able to share that she was scared of her father and thought he might come and find her and see her book. Her social worker reassured her that she was safe and that her father was not allowed to see her or her book – she wanted the picture to stay covered up and they agreed to do this, mindful of the need to go at her pace and help her to feel safe.

Life-story work will create a foundation for your child to understand their history and help prepare them for the next part of their story (Rees 2009; Ryan and Walker 2007).

Goodbyes

As well as preparing to move by gaining a sense of their history, your child will need help to say their goodbyes. Careful consideration needs to be given to the timing of their final goodbye contact with their birth family. To have a 'good goodbye', everyone involved needs to prepare for the meeting rather than just all turning up at a contact centre with the children playing and the adults having a cup of tea without acknowledging the significance and the emotional intensity of this meeting. Each family member needs their own support so they can acknowledge and process the emotions of the event. Even small children will sense the tension and sadness of the meeting and need sensitive support, keeping to their routine and having their carer with them. They also need a clear message that this is a final goodbye, not a 'goodbye for now ' or a 'see you later', which can leave them muddled and confused. Sometimes these meetings are rushed or the significance ignored, as it is painful and sad. Planning them and preparing with everyone who is going to be there can help the visit to go better. Thinking with the birth parents about how they might feel when they arrive, what they might want to say and if they want to bring a last token present to give their child can help birth parents feel prepared and able to manage this last goodbye rather than feeling overwhelmed or avoiding it by not turning up. Taking photographs can help both children and adults process the goodbye and to place it in the context of all that has happened to get to this point. Given the emotional intensity of final goodbyes, it makes sense for these to be timed appropriately – to avoid being confused saying goodbye to their foster carers and meeting their new parents.

Saying goodbye to their foster carers is a crucial part of the preparation for your child to move – they need to be able to acknowledge the loss of their current attachment figure or they may struggle to accept you as their new attachment figure. The work needs to be planned at the child's pace – if it is hurried or pushed to fit with the agenda of the adults, your child may feel increasingly anxious or stressed. They will be more likely to be sad and angry with you as their new adoptive parents rather than resolving these feelings about leaving before they go (Gray 2012b). This goodbye may also trigger a sense of grief connected to all the other losses they have experienced, so an awareness of their history needs to be part of the work.

Your child will need support from their social worker and their foster carer to be able to share their sense of loss. They will need clear information about the plans and why this loss is happening – they may rather stay where they are rather than face any more change as they feel safe and settled now. They may think it is their own fault that they are moving again and will need to know they are moving as a result of the adults' making decisions to keep them safe, rather than because of something they may have done or thought (Fahlberg 2012).

Charlotte, aged six, was going with her adoptive mother to her swimming lesson when she asked her mother why she had bought her and not another baby. She had moved at the age of two and had shown no sign of distress or sadness on leaving her foster carer. Charlotte seemed to have been unable to process her grief at leaving them and had created her own explanation as to why she had to leave.

Adults may want to hurry a move due to all sorts of pressures – bureaucratic, financial and emotional – but for the move to be successful, your child needs time to grieve their losses. This starts with their social worker and foster carer supporting them to understand their loss and to express their feelings about it. They may use stories and time to draw and play out their losses to help your child express their anger and sadness. They may reflect on the time spent living with your child's foster carer; creating a treasure chest of keep-sakes and putting together memory books with photos of the people and events that have been important to them. Doing these activities with their foster family gives them opportunities to reflect on the things they will miss and their sadness at saying goodbye (Gray 2012b; Siegel and Hartzell 2004).

Their foster carer plays a hugely significant role in helping your child to grieve – and they need their own support to be able to do this. These events may trigger memories of their own losses, which they might need help with. They will experience their own acute sadness at saying goodbye to a child they have cared for and become close to. If the foster carer is overwhelmed by their own sadness, they may struggle to support your child – and this can sometimes be overlooked as the preparations focus on the child. For first-time foster carers this can be particularly challenging if they are not offered support as they may be unsure how to behave – should they show their sadness or put a brave face on, are some tears OK or should they be upbeat and smile through the goodbye?

Foster carers develop their own ways of saying goodbye and social workers can offer guidance as to the best way to manage this. Some foster families hold a big party to allow their whole family to say goodbye. The timing of this needs careful thinking about so it isn't too overwhelming. Children also have to say goodbye to their school, teachers and friends and too many goodbyes too close together can overwhelm them. This may show in their behaviour as they communicate their anxiety and distress. Other foster families hold a goodbye picnic or have a special family meal to give everyone a chance to celebrate the move, as well as mark your child's leaving. Some give presents and tokens to represent the special times they have spent together. Foster siblings might receive a present from the child to mark this goodbye, as they too will be dealing with the impending departure of someone they may have come to regard as their brother or sister. Some foster families create special rituals for their goodbye meal, which help all the children to say goodbye – they might each light a candle and make a wish for the one who is leaving or make a collage or photograph collection together to represent their time as part of this family.

However well this process has been undertaken, your child will still carry with them this sense of sadness – it is inextricably linked with their history. Research shows that having a trusted adult to support them will help a child grieve, as will a stable and consistent environment and a place where they can share their feelings and talk about the people and the things that they miss (Gray 2012b; Siegel and Hartzell 2004). Your challenge as their adoptive parent is to take over the role as their trusted adult from their foster carer and to provide them with this stable and consistent family environment within which they can share their sadness. You can ensure that their new family life is predictable and consistent and you can help them share their feelings as you build your relationship. Ask questions and be curious about how they might be feeling. Such questions include: 'I know you lived with Ann for two years when she was your foster carer. I wonder what you miss about her house?' or, 'You lived with John and Lorna before you came to live with me – I am sure you miss them and think you would like to visit them.' This will give your child the opportunity to share their feelings about their loss and will give them the message that you are comfortable with talking about the people that they miss.

Their grief may return in waves as they settle in with you. It can be triggered by certain times of the year or events such as holidays or birthdays that remind them of their birth family or foster carers. Note when the introductions happened and what the weather was like and whether anything was happening around that time as these can all be clues in the future as to when your child might struggle. This is one reason why moving at Christmas or near their birthday is not a good idea as these events become associated with moving, sadness and anxiety. Your child may seem unsettled, sleep less well, seem grumpy or sad and need help to feel better again (Gray 2012a).

Preparing to move and looking forward

The third stage of the preparatory work involves looking forward to living with a new family. This work can be interwoven with the other stages helping your child to understand why they are moving and what this will mean for them, thinking about their worries and questions and preparing them to meet their new parents.

If brothers and sisters are moving together they still need individual time to process their own thoughts and feelings about the move, as well as time spent as a group to share their ideas about going to live with a new family (Saunders, Selwyn, Fursland 2013).

Older children may need separate sessions as they need more detail and may have questions that their younger siblings are not yet old enough to be concerned with. By using books, drawings and playing out moving to a new family, they can share their growing understanding of their story and the plans for their future.

Daisy aged three, and Daniel, aged seven, had lived with their foster carers Gill and Gavin for two years. Gill and Gavin were struggling to help the children prepare for Daisy's adoption. Daniel was going to remain with them. The social worker brought the children a story about two bears and gave them a teddy bear each to hold while she read them the story. She asked both Gill and Gavin to listen too and they sat Daisy and Daniel on their laps. Gavin had been reluctant to take part as he said he didn't normally get involved with the meetings to do with the children. The social worker acknowledged that it was hard to be part of this but explained that he was needed to help the children share their sadness and prepare for Daisy to leave.

The story went as follows:

Once upon a time there were two little bears that lived with mummy bear and daddy bear in the middle of the wood in a little house. Sometimes daddy bear shouted at mummy bear and she cried and forgot to make the little bears their tea. The little bears were frightened and hid under the bed until the shouting stopped. One night mummy and daddy bear went out and they did not come back. In the morning, the two little bears went out into the woods to look for some food and they were found wandering in the woods by the Wise Owl. He took them to stay with Mr and Mrs Brown Bear who lived on the other side of the woods. The little bears were given some tea and then they stayed with the Brown Bears while the Wise Owl thought about what to do.

After a while the Wise Owl came to visit the little bears and told them his plan – he wanted them to be safe and looked after until they were big bears and they both needed a mummy bear and a daddy bear who knew how to look after little bears. He had decided that one little bear would go and live with Mr and Mrs Snowy Bear who lived in the mountains and knew how to look after little bears. The other little bear would stay with Mr and Mrs Brown Bear, as they also knew how to look after little bears. So both little bears would grow up safely and every third Sunday they would meet in the middle of the woods to play and have tea together. And this is what they did and they all lived happily ever after.

After the story and a snack, Daisy and Daniel played moving families with the social worker and their foster carers using the bears and lots of cushions. The social worker wondered out loud about how the bears might be worried they wouldn't get to see each other again and that they might be sad and miss playing together in the woods. Daniel's bear was worried that Daisy's bear wouldn't get her favourite food to eat and wanted her bear to stay with his – and so they continued to play to explore their worries about Daisy's move.

Other stories can explore worries about being naughty, missing people, feeling sad or feeling cross – playing out these themes with the grown-ups supporting them to move can help your child untangle the confusion, muddles and feelings about their own story. Social workers can write their own stories or use books that reflect these themes to focus on particular issues that they think your child might struggle with, given their individual history. Sharing this work between the foster carer, and then with you as their adopter, builds a connection between all the adults caring for your child and helps them move forward.

Connecting up the work they have done about their past with their future plans helps develop your child's sense of a coherent story – in line with Rees' model (2009), they are still grounded in the present while looking back before looking forwards.

Asking children what they would like in a new family can lead to some highly unrealistic requests for horses, swimming pools and helicopter pads! It can be a good way of engaging children in the work but needs to be tempered by a sense of the adults being responsible for the choices that will be made. It is helpful to enable a child to feel involved in the process but the key message they need is that the grown-ups are responsible for making sure they find a family where they can live safely and be looked after until they are grown-up. The social worker describing your adoptive family to the child needs to be mindful of their history – calling you their 'forever family' is meaningless if the child has moved more times than they can remember. They have been hurt and let down by the people who 'loved and cared' for them in the past – telling a child they are joining a new family can evoke feelings of panic and anxiety rather than excitement and joy. Your child's expectation of this new plan may be profoundly influenced by their previous experiences and their internal working models of grown-ups and how they behave. Acknowledging this mismatch is part of the work to explore children's worries and fears. Playing out the plans using puppets and reading stories about children and animals in difficult situations who are helped to live happily ever after can help with younger children. Older children can read these stories with their foster carers and have the chance to think about their own story.

Compiling a notebook to share with you as their adopters is another good way to help older children prepare to move –

sometimes it is called their 'wishes and worries book'. This is to help your child think about some of the things they really want their adopters to know about them. The notebook can include pictures and their own writing to introduce themselves, their hobbies and favourite things to do, what they are afraid of and what they like or hate to eat. They can create their own book for introductions similar to the one you as their adopters will make for them. Choosing what they will put in the book gives them a sense of ownership and some control over the process. The book can also be used to let you know some of their worries and questions before they come and live with you – they might ask what kind of food you cook, how they will get to school, what happens if they do something naughty, what happens if they wet the bed and if you know their 'real' story.

When you meet your child you can answer their questions and acknowledge the worries that they may have about moving to live with you (Gray 2012b). Foster carers can help make these books – putting in photographs of the things that everyone in their family enjoys doing together, such as walking the dog and Friday film and pizza nights, and they can help with sharing who is who in their family. The foster carer joining in with this piece of work is another signal to the child that they are supporting their move and want it to be successful.

> Sophie, Ethan and Jonnie, aged eight, six and five, were about to start introductions to their new mum and dad. The children had spent the first four years of their lives living in a dirty and chaotic house. Their birth mother was an alcoholic and had had several different partners. Sophie had done most of the caring for her brothers and her sense of responsibility for them had persisted in foster care. For their adopters, Ethan and Jonnie made books full of their favourite things with drawings of pizzas, their local park and going swimming. Sophie's book talked about her favourite things and how she was looking forward to having time with a new mum and not having to 'be big all the time'. But she also stuck in a letter full of worries and questions about what

might happen if the boys were naughty: would she still see her foster carer, what would happen if she lost her school bag, what would happen if she broke something as she was a clumsy girl, what if things went wrong?

Preparing these books can help children voice their anxieties before the move and give you an insight into their world before they join your family. They can form part of the ongoing work that they will do to help them make the transition to your family.

CHAPTER SIX

· · · · · · · · · ·

When Everyone is Ready

More about introductions

Introductions are for you to get to know each other and to start building an attachment relationship between you and your child. The introductions will start at the foster carer's home, as this is your child's secure base. Your child will be helped to make the transition from their foster carer's care to yours – starting with being in a familiar place when they meet you, but with their foster carer still caring for them in familiar surroundings. As your child begins to get to know you, their foster carer will guide you in caring for your child. As the transition process progresses, you will take over more and more of the parenting role as the foster carer steps back, but remains available to support you all.

Time to move

When all the preparations are complete and everyone is ready for the next stage, you will be invited to a planning meeting which will outline in detail the actual introductions between you and your child. With some organisations you will meet your child before this meeting takes place, while with others you will meet them after this meeting. The timings for every part of this process are crucial to its success and will be tailored to the individual needs of each child. The move needs to be achieved with the least shock, trauma and disruption to your child. If introductions are too fast then your child may go into shock, which can then interfere with their future attachment relationships with you. They may feel frightened and anxious as they lose the trusted attachment figure of their foster carer. They are vulnerable – given their past experiences of loss and trauma – to being overwhelmed by anxiety and unable to trust that you as their new parents will take care of them. They may blame themselves for the move – identifying things that they have done as the cause of this disruption to their life. Their sense of loss may engulf them as they leave their foster family and possibly their siblings (Gray 2012b).

To help them move well, timing is critical to planning introductions. Your child needs enough time to understand the move, through preparation and life-story work appropriate to their age, developmental stage and history. They need enough time to grieve and they need support to express their feelings, so they can feel sad but not be overwhelmed by grief. They need enough time to begin to know you as their adoptive parents who will then help them to manage their feelings and the move to join your family.

Telling children too early about the plans for them to move to an adoptive family can be unhelpful – young children do not have a well-developed sense of time, of how long things take or of the time between things happening so if they are told too early and there is a long gap before anything happens, they will fill the gap with anxiety.

Gray suggests using very simple direct language such as 'lots and lots of days' to explain the plan to very young children (Gray 2012b, p.266). Older children can use a countdown calendar to help them understand the timescales for their move. They can fill in the dates for goodbye visits to their school and with their foster carers, the first meeting with their adopters and the visits planned to their home to give them a clear and concrete framework for the move.

The key when planning introductions is not to rush them – spending two weeks in introductions or less for a baby is common practice. However, each child brings a complex history and needs for attachment and may require longer – older children in particular may need three weeks or more to develop a relationship with their adopters before they are ready to move.

There may be adult factors that influence the planning, for example, when adopters live far way and only have a limited amount of adoption leave, or when foster carers have booked a holiday for after the child has moved. Long introductions may place additional stresses, both practical and emotional, on all the adults involved. However, longer timescales need to be focused on what is right for the individual child. For a particular child or sibling group, the timescales may need to be extended. Older children, children with complex histories and attachment needs and sibling groups may need timescales longer than ten days to two weeks. Taking plenty of time in the beginning enables the child to gradually start building their attachment relationships and not be overwhelmed by panic or anxiety. They will be less likely to be triggered into traumatised behaviour or shock and less likely to lose the developmental milestones they have already achieved. If the process is unhurried, they are less likely to be triggered into a state of self-reliance or state of threat when their fight/flight/freeze survival states are triggered (Burnell 2009; Gray 2012b).

Conversely, if the introductions go on for too long, this can be too hard for everyone. The child may experience a sense of divided loyalties when they are unsure who to go to for care and they cannot complete their grieving process until they move.

For the adults, remaining in this stage of the relationship for too long is stressful and can make other demands hard to manage, in particular the needs of other children who also need to be cared for and thought about as the introductions proceed.

Your child needs to experience meeting you in an environment which is safe and predictable, where they are already nurtured and cared for and can have fun and learn about you as the new people who will look after them. If all the adults can work together to give them this experience, it will be a shared experience which will help them to transfer their attachment relationship from their foster carers to you as their adopters.

Placing sibling groups

Planning introductions for siblings needs to take account of their ages, developmental needs and the dynamics of being a sibling group rather than just a single child. One of the key issues is whether to place siblings all at the same time or to place them one by one.

When brothers and sisters are placed together at the same time, this may mirror their experience in foster care as they will already have established a pattern as a sibling group. Placing them at the same time prevents any 'pecking order' or jealousy arising. Children who have always lived together, particularly very small children, may be extremely distressed if they are suddenly separated when one moves without the other.

If siblings are all placed at the same time you might find it hard to have any one-to-one time with each child and find it exhausting trying to meet all their individual needs. There is also a risk that one child will be overlooked or you might miss their cues that they need your attention if another child is more overtly demanding of your attention. Spend some time thinking about their attachment patterns before they came to you and how they signal their needs – and how this might be affected by being a sibling. You might discover one sibling is much more self-reliant than the other who seeks out your attention and you will need to remember this when you are trying to build an attachment relationship with both of them. Other sibling groups may have developed very strong bonds with each other as a way of surviving their early trauma. They may have a stronger sense of loyalty to each other than to you as an unknown adult. One child may have taken on the role of 'parentified child' and see their role as that of parent to their younger siblings. In your home they may want to continue in this role and may struggle with you over who does the looking after when their siblings need care. This can be a challenge in terms of making your own connection with each child. Spending time with each child individually will help build the relationship. In times of stress they may seek each other out rather than a grown-up as, in their world, they have not been able to rely on the grown-ups around them to take care of them in the past. Your task will be to teach them that they can rely on you to keep them safe.

> Sharanjit and James adopted Katy, aged two and Joseph, aged one. The children had always lived together in the same foster placement and the social worker wanted them to move together to live with Sharanjit and James. On the way over to their first meeting, Sharanjit expressed some qualms about managing two such young children, thinking that it would be almost like having twins. She worried about how they would cope with the foster carer watching them parent for the first time. The foster carer set her at ease straightaway as she talked them through the children's routines. She had organised everything so that all Sharanjit and James had to do was concentrate on getting to know the children. The foster carer made lunch for all of them, so Sharanjit and James could watch how she managed Katy's demands for pudding over anything else and how she began to feed Joseph with his special spoon. At bath-time she directed them to hold the towels and wrap the children up tight ready for their pyjamas before putting them in their cots. They spent a week at the foster carer's house before taking the children home. They stuck to Joseph's routine and he seemed to settle well. Katy seemed more anxious and

would call for her brother each time she noticed he wasn't in the room with her. Sharanjit decided to keep them in the same bedroom just as they had been at the foster carers' home. She asked her mother to keep them supplied with meals while they focused on getting to know the children and spent lots of time reassuring Katy that she and her brother were both safe with them.

For other siblings, it may be more appropriate to place them in a consecutive order, using their birth order to plan who moves in first, following the natural pattern of having one child at a time. This gives you the opportunity to get to know the first one to arrive and have more one-to-one time with them before the next child arrives. This can be especially positive if there is a big age gap between the siblings or if one has more needs or difficulties identified before they move. Other siblings may move from different foster carers to be together – they might spend time having sleepovers at each other's homes before moving in together rather than one moving to the other's foster home. Siblings who have been in different foster homes need to get to know each other, but the number of moves should be minimised. The first meeting needs to involve everyone to avoid there being any sense of favouritism and jealousy, which can be intensified by sibling rivalry. If one child then moves in first, the other child will need to have visits planned to start the process of building their relationship with the family. Once they are all home, then the real work of building their sense of being part of your family can begin. This is the time to call on your support network for practical and emotional assistance to help you meet the demands made on you by children who are just learning about how to be part of your family (Burnell 2009; Saunders *et al.* 2013).

If you already have a child

If you already have children, their needs also need to be taken into account when planning introductions. Keeping their routines and activities as much the same as possible will help them feel calm and less anxious. Spend time with them to give them the opportunity to share how they are feeling. They can feel left out of the process and then suddenly have a new brother or sister who takes up a lot of your time and attention and the reality may not be as positive as their fantasy about having a new sibling. You may feel torn between wanting to make sure that they are all right and getting to know your new child. Introductions need to include them from as early a stage as possible to help them feel part of the process. They need a clear explanation of why you need to visit on your own first, so they don't feel excluded. Encourage them to choose activities to take to introductions and for the first few days at home to help them take an active role in the introductions. They might also benefit from having a visual timetable for the plan so they have a clear sense of what is happening and when. Remember, especially if your older child was also adopted, that introductions may trigger memories and feelings linked to their own experience of being adopted; they may need time to explore these with your support. They may need extra reassurance that you love them and have enough love for everyone. They may need to be told that their place in your family is secure. Watching someone new unpack their things in their house may remind them of the moves they have made in the past and lead to them feeling anxious and upset without being able to name why they feel that way – they are experiencing triggers to their own past experience. Talk to them about your memories of when they first came to live with you to help them make sense of their own story and what this new experience is triggering for them. Sometimes you may need to alter the plans for introductions to make sure that their needs are balanced with the needs of your new child. Talk with your social worker to make sure that their needs are also the focus of the plans.

Dave and Jonathan had adopted Jake three years previously when he was four. Now aged seven, he was about to become a big brother to Ryan, aged two. During introductions, Dave and Jonathan were careful to include Jake in all the preparations, taking him to shop for Ryan's new bedroom and letting him choose the quilt cover for Ryan's bed and a new one for his 'big brother' bed. They did some work with him and their social worker, preparing him for the big change and he was excited about having a brother to play football with. The introductions plan was complicated as they wanted to keep Jake's routine as consistent as possible. The first few visits were timed so that they could be back to collect Jake from school. They took him along on the third visit so he could meet Ryan and give him the teddy he had chosen for him. Then they both took Jake home so they could hear how he felt about meeting Ryan. They took turns to be at Ryan's bedtime routine, so that the other could be at home with Jake and put him to bed. It was an exhausting week with lots of driving back and forth for Dave and Jonathan, but they were aware of Jake's need for their presence as much as Ryan's. The first visit home went well with the boys running around the house together. Dave took Ryan back to his foster carers while Jonathan stayed to make tea for Jake. During tea, Jake became grumpier and grumpier and had a tantrum, refusing to go to bed. When Jonathan finally got to the bottom of it, he had to reassure Jake that Ryan was coming back to stay. Ryan's going back to the foster carers had triggered memories for Jake of moving between carers before he lived with Dave and Jonathan and he felt confused and anxious. Jonathan reassured him about the plans and they settled down together to read a story and wait for Dave to come home.

Start of introductions

After all the preparatory work, your social worker and the foster carer will tell your child that they have found them the right new parents who will look after them until they are grown-up. How much they tell them will depend on how old your child is and their story so far. They will show them your photographs and talk about the plans for the move. The foster carer will use the photographs to build up the child's familiarity with you – some foster carers put up the photos in their house or next to your child's bed, some encourage the child to say 'goodnight' to their new mummy and daddy as they create the story of their move to live with their new parents. The foster carer will talk a lot about what will happen so the plan becomes familiar. The foster carer's role in this last piece of preparation is crucial as they convey their sense of the move as a positive thing which they support, while acknowledging that it will be sad and scary to move.

> Tricia had fostered Blake, aged three, for a year and he was due to meet his adoptive parents, Jenny and Paul, the following week. She copied the adopters' photographs onto a placemat for Blake's bowl and one onto his pillowcase. As they played together she talked to him about the plan and what would happen – that his new mummy and daddy would be coming soon to see him and that they would be in Tricia's house a lot. They would feed and bathe him, play with him and maybe even cook his tea in her kitchen. Tricia reassured him that she would not be going anywhere and would stay there all the time. She told him that he might feel scared or wobbly in his tummy but that was OK. It would be an exciting time to meet his new mummy and daddy but it might feel scary too. She also told him that she would always think about him as special to her, but she was really happy that he had a new mummy and daddy that he could stay with until he was big. His adopters had sent him a teddy bear and she encouraged him to carry it around with him.

As introductions begin, there is a huge amount of sharing between the foster carers and you as your child's new parents. The social worker can help you to acquire all the information you need to help you parent consistently by arranging sessions for you to talk with the foster carer. You may not like or agree with the way that the foster carer does everything, from what she feeds your child to how she organises their bedtime routine, but your child will feel safer if their new environment and routine mirror their old one as closely as possible. These sessions are also an opportunity to learn more of your child's personality and history and all the little details that won't have been recorded such as their favourite nursery rhymes, and how they like to have their feet tickled. The more information and the clearer sense of their routine you have, the more confident you will feel. These sessions can also be a time to explore scenarios and how to manage any difficulties you may encounter. Ask the foster carer how they manage if your child has a temper tantrum or what they do to calm them down when they are upset.

> Blake's adopters telephoned Tricia from the park – he kept running away and they were worried he wouldn't come back to them. Tricia explained that they needed to be clear and firm with Blake and tell him that he had to hold onto the pushchair or their hand, but he could not run off on his own. With that advice they were able to manage the rest of the afternoon in the park and he responded well to their confident parenting. Tricia was happy to support them in developing their parenting and also helped them to recognise that Blake needed firm boundaries to help him feel safe with them.

The foster carer can tell you what she thinks your child might struggle with and how they might behave during the first meetings. An acknowledgment by everyone involved of the intensity of what is to come – with your anxiety to get it right and their anxiety that it will go well for all of you – can help the process go more smoothly. There may well be things that don't go so well and agreeing to talk about these times as they arise can help. Consider how you will all respond if your child is naughty or upset, if they refuse to go to you or if they won't do as they are asked. Reflecting together on the feelings your child may be communicating about the process and understanding that they may be feeling fear, rejection and unsafe can guide you in your responses to them. The foster carer will give you feedback on how they think things are going and your social worker will help you work through any difficulties.

> Once back from the park, Tricia noticed that Jenny looked exhausted and seemed quiet. She asked her if she wanted a cup of tea and they went into the kitchen. She asked how the outing had gone and Jenny described how Blake had run over to another woman by the swings and put his arms out to be picked up. Jenny described feeling worried that she wouldn't be able to make a connection with Blake, as he seemed happy to go to anyone that was near him. They talked about Blake's early life and Tricia remembered what Blake had been like when he had first been placed in foster care – he would smile at anyone who came to the house and happily sit on their lap rather than go to Tricia for a cuddle. Jenny's social worker joined them and they talked over Jenny's worries. She reminded them of his early history: he had lived with his birth mother in a hostel and she had often left him with people there while she had gone out. His attachment strategy of charming anyone to look after him had been triggered by all the change he was experiencing. To make a more secure attachment, Jenny and Paul would have to offer him repeated experiences of them looking after him as his parents.

At this point, remind your support network of your plans for the first few weeks of introductions and your need for their support. Share your plans with them so they are clear about what you are doing. Ask them to be specific about the support they can offer you – whether they can bring you meals, walk the dog or take your older child to football practice. Identify who you can call if you need to talk – and whether they can be available late at night if you need to talk then. Be clear about how you will keep people up-to-date on how things are going – some new adopters decide just to withdraw from contact for a while, others phone one person who passes on the news. Make sure everyone knows what your plans are about visitors so they don't just drop by to meet the children, but wait to be invited.

First meeting

Although this is often seen as the high point of all the planning and preparation, this moment is also part of a much bigger story which needs to take account of what went before and what is to come. The first meeting is a step along the way in your story as a family. As adopters, you will have waited a long time for this moment and will be well prepared, know your child's history and what you need to give as parents. Your child will have been prepared by their social worker and foster carer to be expecting you – they might be looking out of the window with their carer to see who can spot you first.

First meetings are exciting but also daunting for everyone – take things slowly to allow your child to get to know you gradually. Don't be tempted to rush in; your child's foster carer needs to signal that they are in charge of the hand-over so your child will stay safe. The foster carer will demonstrate in her behaviour that you are people your child can like and trust. They will be encouraged to call you 'mummy' or 'daddy' from the beginning as a sign of your new relationship. Sometimes children have been calling their foster carers mummy and daddy so this can be confusing. The foster carer's social worker might encourage the foster carers to add their first names to begin to differentiate between your child's different sets of parents. If your child uses your first names, this might be disappointing when you have waited so long to be someone's mummy or daddy. Try to bear in mind that they may have had several other 'mummies and daddies' before you and will need time to learn, recognise and trust that you are their parents. Show them that you are their parents by calling each other mummy or daddy and getting those around you to call you this as well rather than using your first names. If you are in a same-sex partnership, decide on the names you will use and let the foster carer know so she can use these, as well as using them in your introductory book.

If your child is old enough, you can also talk about this with them as part of their story – 'I know that you have lived with other people called mummy before coming to live with me and that calling me mummy too might seem strange and give you muddles.' Some adopters have used different words for mother and father to differentiate themselves from their child's previous parents – but it is the relationship that you build up over time that will give these words their meaning, so try not to worry too much in the early days if your child keeps calling you by your first names.

The first meeting is usually no more than an hour. If it all seems to be going well, carers may suggest that you stay longer. But remember that this first face-to-face meeting will be intense and exhausting for your child and it is just the beginning. Adopters who stay longer may see their child becoming increasingly hard to calm – a result of too much, too soon. Be guided by the foster carer in the first meeting so they can signal to the child that this is a safe situation. As the foster carer is your child's attachment figure, they can trust them to keep them safe when meeting you for the first time. The foster carer might give you something to do so that your child can just watch you and get used to you being there. She might ask you to come and help her with something – maybe folding laundry, matching socks or sorting out a jigsaw puzzle, something very ordinary and everyday to enable the child to experience your presence without having to directly interact with you if they are not ready. If you take a present, a simple puzzle or sticker book that you can do together is a good idea – nothing too big or too complicated, as they may struggle to manage the excitement or the challenge.

The foster carer might ask you to sit on the floor to play with a toy and gently encourage your child to join you all. The situation will be less intense if you play first with the foster carer and follow their lead. Be mindful of what you know of your child's history as you see how they engage with you at that first meeting. They might be triggered into a survival response – some children run and hide behind their foster carer rather than join in (flight/freeze), others can get grumpy and get into a squabble with their siblings (fight) and others may act in a very compliant manner (freeze). Notice how they respond to their foster carer and to you in that first set of interactions – they may be very clingy to their foster carer and follow her as she goes to put the kettle on (anxious attachment); they may choose a different toy to the one you are playing with and resist your best efforts to get them to join in with you or refuse help when they are struggling with the new game (self-reliant, avoidant attachment pattern); they may come straight over to you, sit on your lap and monopolise your attention (indiscriminate, anxious attachment). Be curious about how they are responding to you and consider what might have been triggered for them as a result of their early experiences as they meet you. Notice if they behave differently with you and your partner and how this might relate to their previous experiences with adults.

> Isobel came to the front door with her foster carer and introduced herself to Laura and James. 'Hello, I'm Isobel and I am four.' She took James by the hand and they went into the living room where she showed him her toys. She sat and played dolls with him while Laura and the foster carer made drinks. When Laura tried to join in the game, Isobel turned to James and asked him to go out into the garden with her. The others followed them out into the garden and watched as James pushed Isobel on the swing – she shouted 'no' when Laura offered to push her and kept saying 'daddy do it'. Isobel had spent the early years of her life with her birth mother and three older siblings. Her birth mother had mental health and alcohol problems and her birth father had often been absent from the home. In Isobel's world, her mother had not kept her safe or looked after her and she had sometimes been very frightening when she was drunk. Her father had given her lots of attention when he was home but had disappeared for long periods. On meeting her new parents, Isobel reacted to James and Laura in a way that reflected her past experiences. She responded to these

new people she had been told would look after her with
behaviour designed to keep herself safe.

The foster carer will give your child a way out if they need it
during that first meeting. Sometimes adopters put themselves
under pressure in that first visit for it all to go perfectly and
for the child to stay in the room with them the whole time.
If the first meeting gets too intense, your child may need to
follow their foster carer out to the kitchen, have a break and
return when they are ready. Pace the meeting in line with their
emotional readiness to engage with you.

During introductions

As the gradual hand-over of your child's care begins, the foster
carer will continue to play a key role. The process of separation
from the foster carer will start, but they will remain a source of
reassurance and support for your child and can give you guidance
and feedback about how things are going during the transition
period. Over the following days, you will learn more about each
other and begin to establish a connection. Sharing increasing
amounts of time together gives you the opportunity to learn all
the practical details of how to care for your child – practising
bath-time, nappy changing and how to strap them into their
pushchair. Initially, the foster care will show you 'how to', and
this gives you and your child the chance to observe each other
with a safe person mediating your time together. Gradually the
foster carer will give you the parenting tasks, but be on hand to
support you all.

As well as learning the practical side of how to be a parent,
the process of your child leaving their foster carer and beginning
to make an attachment relationship with you begins. Using play
and activities with an attachment focus can help this process. The
games need to be tailored to your child's developmental level,
but using games that are interactive and focus on relationship
building can help create a positive connection between you.
During introductions, try playing together with bubbles and

Play-Doh, build towers and race cars, play hide-and-seek and peekaboo, clapping and singing games and play with your child's dolls to create stories.

Sometimes there is a need during introductions to make some special time to play out your child's story to help them make sense of the move and to share their story with you as their adopters. You might need some support from their social worker and arrange some times to play out their story with their foster carer present to support them. Children who have a difficult story to tell or particular struggles or attachment issues can be helped to make the transition to their adoptive family by giving them this support during introductions. This will follow the life-story work they have already done and can be continued once they have moved. The social worker might bring the toys and stories they have used during the preparation sessions and use these to help tell your child's story. They will support your child to share their feelings about the move in the presence of both you and their foster carer using the toys. This will help them make the transition from their foster carer to you as their new parent in a way that acknowledges and accepts their past. Talking and sharing their story will also help them develop a sense of trust in you as it shows them that you accept them, no matter what has happened in the past. Looking at their life-story book together or talking to them and their foster carers about their life-story during introductions gives your child a sense that all the adults are helping to keep them safe and help them move well, and they do not need to carry a sense of shame about their story into their new family (Norris and Twigger 2013).

> Lizzy was six and had lived with her foster carer, Karen, for two years. She had spent the first four years of her life living with her birth parents who had drug and alcohol issues. Her birth father had seriously injured her birth mother in a fight and Lizzy had been taken into care. She was an extremely anxious child who clung to her foster carer and was worried by any changes to her routine. Lizzy's social worker, Anna, spent lots of time playing with her about her story during the

preparations for her to move to her adoptive family. Anna asked Karen to help prepare Lizzy and they all played games together. Lizzy's favourite game was hide-and-seek and they played that a lot. Anna wrote a story which they acted out with puppets about a scary mummy and daddy fighting a lot and then the policeman came and took the baby to live with a safe mummy and daddy. When Lizzy's new mummy and daddy came to meet her, Anna was there and asked everyone to play some games together to help Lizzy get to know her new mummy and daddy. On their next visit, Anna brought the puppets and they acted out the story again for Lizzy's new mummy and daddy to watch. Anna brought her toys with her to visit Lizzy in her new home and they played together about being a new family for Lizzy.

The pace of introductions will vary according to your child's needs. Children under three have not developed a sense of time, so they need more frequent visits over a shorter timeframe. These will take place primarily in the foster carer's home before the child moves. Children over three are more able to separate temporarily from their attachment figure and have developed a sense of leaving and returning, so they can go out with you to the park and come back to their foster carer, just as they go to nursery or playgroup and come back. In the plan there will be times for going out to the park or to a café and then returning, so there are opportunities for you to take over parenting. At these times be mindful of your child's need for safety and the heightened anxiety that they will feel. If they have insecure attachment patterns, they may struggle with leaving their attachment figure. Going out with you may trigger memories for them of leaving other parent figures, of being abandoned or leaving a parent and then not seeing them again. They may remember being taken out by strangers and not kept safe. First outings need to be short and not rushed if your child is showing distress at leaving their attachment figure (Fahlberg 2012; Gray 2012b).

Talking about the plan is also important even if they are little – 'we are going to go to the swings for half an hour and

Linda is going to stay here and make us some sandwiches. You might feel a bit wobbly in your tummy going out without her but you can hold my hand and we will come back to Linda when it's lunchtime.'

> Tilly had fostered Jemima, aged three, for two years. When her adopters Sue and Sarah met her for the first time, she asked them in and sat them at the table with a cup of tea and Jemima's favourite puzzle. Jemima initially hid behind Tilly but they kept chatting and putting out the puzzle bits and she eventually stood in between Sue and Tilly to help put the puzzle together. The first time they went to the park, Jemima held Tilly's hand all the way there and then on the way back she held Tilly and Sarah's hand. On the next trip out, Tilly suggested that Sue and Sarah take Jemima to the swings while she had some tea in the café. Sue and Sarah came rushing to find her as Jemima had fallen off the swing and was calling for Tilly. Tilly calmed her down and they all walked back to the swings. The next day, Tilly told them she was taking her sons out for lunch and they could make some sandwiches for themselves as there was plenty in the fridge, and so Sue and Sarah gradually took over Jemima's care. They were able to appreciate how much Jemima needed Tilly, as her attachment figure, when she was anxious or hurt and responded to her need to have Tilly near her during the introductions without rushing her to let them look after her.

The foster carer plays a key role in giving your child the message that you are safe to trust and like, and that, in contrast to other grown ups they have lived with, you are safe and can take care of them. They will show that they are in charge of keeping your child safe and looking after them and will hand this responsibility over to you as their new attachment figures. Your child needs the opportunity to develop these new attachments and, if they are started well with the support of the foster carer, then the transition will be positive. You need to be available 'on demand' to make emotional connections just as you would with a baby; this can be exhausting and overwhelming. Use your social worker and family to share the ups and downs as you go through introductions to help you make sense of your experiences and how you are feeling.

Follow the foster carer's lead and learn from them as you move from playing side by side to more intense engagement. Notice how your child responds and consider what they may be communicating through their behaviour. Rather than a rush to intimacy, they may need a slower pace to build up your relationship. Adopters sometimes voice a worry about not 'loving' their child at the beginning and being unsure of what to say or feel. You are all strangers who are getting to know one another and it is hoped in time you will create bonds of love between you. In the beginning, you might have fallen in love with your child's picture or love the idea of being their parent and find them adorable when you meet them, but the feelings between you will take time and experience to develop. If you are in a partnership, one of you might declare you fell in love with your child the minute you saw them, whereas the other might feel nothing so deeply at the beginning or struggle to feel close to them, particularly if they are going to one of you more of the time. Acknowledge between you that there are differences in how you feel and allow time for these emotions to develop in your relationships without putting yourselves under pressure to feel the 'right' thing.

Some parts of introductions can make children feel more vulnerable and need thinking about to ensure they feel safe. Being taken out can raise a child's anxiety – they may associate particular places such as the local café with going for contact visits or may worry about where they are going and whether they will be taken back to their foster carer. What might look like a great place to take them – such as a soft-play area – may be too busy and noisy and feel unsafe when they are already in a state of heightened anxiety. If the local area is unfamiliar, ask the foster carer to recommend places that are close by to avoid long car journeys and getting lost as this can raise everyone's anxiety. Look for places that offer simple and safe spaces to enjoy spending time together, rather than being worried that they will run off and get hurt or lost. Children who have indiscriminate attachment may readily go off with a stranger and not look to you as their carer as this relationship is still new to them; they need a very close level of supervision to keep them safe when you take them out.

Bath-time can be a vulnerable time for a child as there may be up to three adults in the room and the child is naked. It may remind them of times when they were left alone in the bath and not safe, or times when they were hurt or abused. They may have only ever been bathed by the female foster carer and suddenly adoptive dad wants to help. Taking it in turns to help with bath-time can lessen the anxiety. The foster carer can direct dad to hold the towel or play with the ducks to signal that this is a safe person who can take care of them.

Changes in routines and being in new places can create a sense of confusion for them. Going to your house for tea and then returning to their foster carer's home in their pyjamas makes little sense if they usually put their nightclothes on before going up to their bed. They may have been removed from their birth parents at night and going out to a car in pyjamas may trigger a memory of their past experience which will create feelings of anxiety and fear. You may read them a story and give them a kiss goodnight when they are tucked up in bed. However, with their foster carers they may always have read a story and said goodnight downstairs so they may be unsure about what may happen when they are upstairs. Use the plan to explore with your child what might be different. Talk to them about how it might make them feel confused, and reassure them that you will keep them safe.

If the plans go too fast or the child is overwhelmed by the loss and change that they are experiencing, they may present behaviour that the foster carer may not have seen since they were placed with them. They may be grumpy, sleep or eat poorly. They may have temper tantrums or constantly ask for the foster carer and reject your attempts to take care of them. They are signalling that they are struggling and the adults need to take time to reflect on how best to support them to manage the move. Creating a sense of safety for them with order, structure and routine, and opportunities to acknowledge with them how hard and how sad this process is for them can help the transition.

As the days go by, you will take over more and more of the care-giving. You will see how the foster carer manages 'no' and discipline and how they soothe your child when they are distressed. Copy their tone of voice and their responses as you take over calming them and helping them with their distress. As they develop a growing sense that there is change happening, your child may present behaviour which reflects unease with the change. A small baby may become more fretful and harder to soothe, toddlers may have more and bigger tantrums and older children may become sulky and grumpy. Try to remember the feelings beneath their behaviour – they need boundaries and discipline, but it needs to be overlaid with empathy for their struggles as they leave their carer and their familiar life. In times of stress, which is what it will be for them when they are with you, they will feel confused and anxious. Instead of the internal working model of the world developed with their foster carers of adults as safe and caring, their first internal working model of the world which was shaped by their experiences of living with their birth parents – of adults as hurtful and neglectful – will resurface and influence their responses to you. They will need repeated reassurance and soothing from you to help them to recreate a safer and more positive internal working model based on their experiences with you (Kaniuk, Steele and Hodges 2004).

When they come to your house the dynamics shift – the foster carer may bring your child for their first visit but now they will be your guest and you will take over the parent role. When your child comes to your home, use the toys and their things that you have been transferring from the foster carer's house to create a sense of familiarity. Touching and smelling their own teddies and blankets on their new bed and seeing their toys in your living room will give your child reassuring sensory experiences which remind them of their foster home where they felt safe. Seeing their Wellington boots by your back door and their coat hanging next to yours in the hallway shows them that they have a place in your house. Keep the visits low-key and try to stick to their usual routine for meals and playtime. Try to prevent any unexpected visitors dropping by as this may trigger a surge of anxiety. Your child will not feel secure with you at this stage and may worry that this new person visiting might just take them away to somewhere unknown. Children with a history of sudden moves from their birth parents and who have had to move from foster placements in an emergency or who have experienced a placement disruption are particularly vulnerable to this sense that they might be moved at any time. It might be a struggle to take them back to the foster carer's home if they have settled in and had a good day. They may be tired and want to sleep at your house and struggle with the disruption to their usual routine, but help them to know that they will be coming back to your house using their visual timetable and talking with them about what is happening: 'It must be really hard to go back to Jane's house today when you want to sleep in your new bed. We are going to take you back and tuck you in at her house and then tomorrow we will be there in the morning to bring you back here and we will play with your trainset.' Give them reassurance about the plan and talk about what they might be finding hard about the process.

A rest day is sometimes planned towards the end of the introductions to give everyone a chance to take a breath before the final move. For some children such as very young babies it is not necessary, but it gives others a chance to say goodbye and rest before the final move. Foster carers often use this day to have a final farewell, inviting friends and family over to wish your child well. Having a big party or get-together at this stage needs to be balanced with how much the child is having to cope with during introductions and they may struggle with lots of people saying goodbye to them all at once. Other foster families spend the day quietly pottering about using familiar routines as another way to prepare your child for the last day. They use the day to reflect on the child's time with their family, placing it in the context of their broader life history. Having this day allows all the members of the foster family to say goodbye and to wish your child well, acknowledging the significance of their having been part of their family. If there are other children in the foster family, it is really important to include them in the day to enable them to say their goodbyes and grieve the loss that they will experience as the child leaves their family (Gray 2012b).

The foster parents might organise some activities for the last day to help all the children say farewell and to give your child the key messages that they were valued as part of the family, that they will not be forgotten and they wish them well in their new family. They might arrange a special meal with their favourite foods and while they are all round the table, everyone may have a chance to share their memories of the child's time with them, the trips they went on, what they were like when they first came and all the times they have enjoyed together. Other families go on a picnic on the last day and bake a special cake to share as they celebrate the child's future and let off balloons with a message tied to them to send them good wishes and say goodbye. Doing all these things together enables your child and the children that are staying to have the opportunity to grieve their loss and share their worries about moving as well as preparing them to move.

The last day

Once all your child's possessions have been moved and all the goodbyes said, you are ready to take your child home with you. This is an emotional time for everyone – there is sadness, anxiety and excitement. The event will have different meanings and significance for those involved. For it to go well, it needs to be well planned and the emotions acknowledged rather than having a hurried goodbye and then just leaving. After all the preparation and planning, you should feel confident and ready to parent your child and they should be ready to leave their foster carer.

Foster carers describe this day with mixed emotions – they are happy that the child they have loved and cared for will have a happy future, which is why they have become a foster carer.

However, saying goodbye is painful and they will naturally worry about whether your child will be all right and whether they will settle quickly. The foster carer needs support to consider how they are going to manage on the day and afterwards. Some want to be left alone once they have said goodbye, others plan to spend the day with their family doing something special, while others plan to meet up with someone they can share their sadness with. Sometimes they struggle to manage the goodbye as they feel ambivalent about the child leaving; perhaps part of them wanted to keep the child, perhaps they have doubts about whether the adopters are the right ones for this child or whether they will manage, or the departure may trigger other unresolved losses for them. They may need additional support from their social worker to help them resolve these feelings.

On the actual day, the hand-over is best kept short and early in the day to enable everyone to manage, without escalating everyone's anxiety levels. It is important not to hurry the goodbyes. Some foster carers want to strap the child into the car seat to signal their support for the plan, whereas others prefer to say goodbye at the front door. They may fear breaking down in front of your child and worry about crying in front of them. Without a sense of this being a real goodbye, the child may be left with a sense of confusion about what is really happening, so foster carers need support to be able to express their sadness and be able to say goodbye rather than avoid it.

As you drive away, you may experience a range of emotions: relief that the introductions are over, guilt that you are taking your child away from their familiar carers, anxiety about how you will cope and the excitement at becoming a family. Consider as you drive that your child will also be experiencing similar feelings of anxiety, excitement and sadness. As you travel to their new home, focus on helping them feel safe; strap them in with a blanket or a toy that smells familiar, sing them songs, play their favourite music in the car and talk to them about how they are feeling and what you will do when you get home.

'What I am really thinking'

Introductions are an intensely emotional process – not just a set of dates, times, places and people. Social workers play a key role in planning, preparing, supporting and mediating between all those involved. Sometimes during introductions there are times when relationships between the key people can become difficult and they need help to manage the issues that arise. Consider the different issues at play as people meet.

As an adopter, what I am really thinking?

- It feels awkward sitting in someone else's house.

- I am really hungry, will we get something to eat?

- Why are they sitting in the kitchen and we are in here?

- I am worried I will get it wrong.

- What if they don't like me or think I can't do it?

- I think they are cross that we were late back from the park.

- The bed-and-breakfast is cold and I miss my own bed.

- I'm worried about my son staying back home with his grandma.

- I miss my dog.

- I feel really sad.

- I don't think they approve of us.

- I feel like I am kidnapping their daughter.

- My partner is bonding better than me; she seems to like him more.

- We shouldn't have given her sweets, now she won't eat her tea.

- I can't wait to be in our home.

- I feel overwhelmed, I should feel more excited.

As a foster carer, what I am really thinking?

- I am not sure they are the right people.

- I would like to keep her.

- I will be so sad to see her go and I will miss her so much.

- I am not sure they stuck to the plan today.

- They were out too long and now he won't go to sleep.

- I am not sure they are ready.

- This is the first time I've done this and I'm not sure I'm saying the right things.

- I am worried their daughter won't like him.

- I think they are being too soft with her.

- My husband thinks he should stay with us.

Such thoughts and feelings can emerge during the introductions and each person needs time and space to reflect on their feelings and the worries they have. The foster carer may struggle with the impending loss and need help to resolve this. They may blame you as the adopters for not doing it right, but actually they may be upset that they are not going to keep this child. They may feel ambivalence about giving up a child who they have become close to – their feelings about the plan and any worries or concerns they may have need exploring so they can support the plan.

As an adopter you may feel uncomfortable having to be in someone else's home, following another person's routines. You may miss having your own family and friends around and the comfort of your own home if you have to stay away. You may blame the foster carer for your own insecurity and lack of confidence if you feel they are judging you. This may reflect your worries about the future and how you will be as a parent. Recognise that this process is exhausting and challenging and that you need to take care of yourselves and make enough time and space to focus on the introductions. Make sure that you are happy with the arrangements for your other children if you have them and that their needs are taken account of when the plans are made.

For introductions to go well, everyone needs to acknowledge the emotional intensity and the significance of the process. The foster carer needs support to be able to manage their vital role. As an adopter it is important to recognise and honour the bond between your child and their foster carers. During the initial meetings, try to identify possible times and issues that might cause difficulties or misunderstandings and think together about how to manage these. Clarify how meals are going to be provided, whether the foster carer expects you to contribute, whether they have other children whose needs also have to be considered in terms of the timetable. Think about what will happen and how it will make people feel if the child runs continually to the foster carer and ignores you, if they refuse to eat their lunch, if they go only to your partner and refuse to let you take care of them, if you are late and their routine is then disrupted. If difficulties arise, or people express concerns about the process, these need to be addressed so that everyone can manage the process in the best way that they can (Fahlberg 2012; Gray 2012b).

So how can you best prepare for the emotional intensity of introductions?

Spend time considering how best to take care of yourself – consider the following:

- Who will be in your support network?

- Which specific things might you need help with? Different people might be able to help with different tasks.

- Who can help care for your other children during introductions?

- Who can you call on in the middle of the night if you need to talk?

- Who can bring you a meal or help with taking the dog out?

Looking after yourself is important – eat well, sleep well, take time to rest and connect with your friends. Adopters have talked about the difficulty of staying in touch with friends when introductions are in full swing – everyone is dying to know how you are getting on but you will be tired and have no time to keep answering the phone. Some people use a blog for their friends and family to keep them updated and others have arranged a texting pyramid to keep everyone in the loop. Others will heed your warning that you will need to focus on the children but will be back in touch when you can.

Identify how you respond to stress – what are the early warning signs that you are starting to feel more stressed? Do you sleep or eat more or less, do you tend to withdraw from being sociable, do you become agitated or irritable and argumentative? Ask your friends or partner – what would they notice if you were struggling? How do you respond to extreme stress – fight, flight or freeze?

Once you have worked out what your response to stress is, make a list of activities and things that help you calm down and make you feel less stressed and more regulated. Some people love massage, some prefer going for a long run or a brisk walk with the dog. There might be particular music that makes you feel calmer and happier, or lighting your favourite scented candle may soothe you. Identify what works for you and let your partner do the same – then make a list and stick it on the fridge so it can act as a reminder in the middle of a busy time.

Spending some time thinking about your own attachment history and your possible vulnerable spots helps prepare you for the emotional challenges you may encounter in the first few weeks. Your child may behave in ways that trigger unexpected and difficult feelings in you; bearing in mind why this behaviour may make you feel the way you do can help you deal with this better. Your child may cling to you and not leave your side – this can leave you feeling suffocated. Your child may go to your partner all the time and reject your care – this can make you feel hurt and angry that they don't want you. Or your child may go to anyone for hugs and avoid you; this may make you feel rejected and a failure as a parent. They may have huge temper tantrums which leave you feeling anxious and unsure how to manage them, or they may hit and hurt you, which may make you cross and reject them. Your child may become very bossy and make you feel unable to keep control.

All these behaviours reflect their attachment patterns and survival strategies, stemming from their early experiences of relationships. They may trigger your own survival strategies and attachment patterns arising from your own family history: how you were soothed when you were unhappy or unwell, how you were disciplined when you were naughty, your sense as a child of being looked after and cared for will shape your responses.

You may notice yourself or your partner becoming very anxious about everything; inexplicably cross over small things or withdrawing from joining in family activities and preferring to be by yourself. None of these responses are surprising given the intensity of new relationships and all our vulnerabilities. But you may need some time and support to explore these feelings so you can develop your understanding of the processes at work and develop a close and secure attachment relationship with your child. Other adopters, your partner or your social worker can all help you to explore these issues and support you (Hughes and Baylin 2012).

CHAPTER SEVEN

• • • • • • • • • • •

Now You are Home

Once the front door is shut, with introductions over and bags unpacked, most adopters feel a huge sense of relief – the awkwardness and intensity of the past few weeks are over and you are back in your own home, and at long last your child is with you. You may also feel a sense of excitement and trepidation – all the months of planning and preparation are finally coming to fruition and you are now a family.

How children feel

Consider how your child might feel on arriving in a new home. They may feel confused and out of sorts, however well they have been prepared and even if they have had good foster care. Moving to a new home – with new adults in a new environment – will trigger anxiety. They may be hypervigilant and alert to any possible signs of threat. They do not have a secure internal model of the world which tells them that this new family will be a good one – only with time and experience will their sense of safety grow, following on from the groundwork of preparation and introductions (Fahlberg 2012).

While you as the grown-up will know that you will meet their needs, they do not know that for sure, given their previous experiences. They will not know whether you will feed them or protect them – or what will happen when they do something wrong or you are cross. They won't know or believe that this family will be their 'forever family' – especially if they have moved several times or lost relationships with people close to them. Young babies and toddlers are often described as being 'too young to know', but research clearly shows that they are affected by their very early experiences of trauma, lack of care and changes in their primary relationships – so even if they move to live with you when they are still little, they will bring with them the impact of this early trauma (Perry *et al.* 1995; Gerhardt 2004).

Some children will arrive having said goodbye to their siblings – they will miss them and may not understand the concept of contact, so they are left with a sense of loss they cannot make sense of. They will also have said goodbye to their foster carers and will be grieving the loss of this relationship. Deborah Gray in *Nurturing Adoptions* (2012b) highlights the importance of acknowledging this grieving process for children – understanding that they will feel sad, angry and confused by their loss before moving to accept it. She identifies that this can be hard for adopters to manage when they want to focus on building their own family relationships. However, supporting children in grieving this sense of loss forms an essential part of becoming a family.

> Josie adopted Molly, aged three. Molly had been with her foster carer, Sue, since she was three days old before moving to live with Josie. During introductions she clung to her foster carer and didn't want to go out without Sue coming too. Once she had moved to Josie's house, Molly kept asking when they were going to see Sue, asking for

her at bedtime and waking up upset in the night. Josie kept reassuring Molly that Sue would be thinking about her and they would meet up soon, but she felt overwhelmed by the intensity of Molly's grief. She wanted to protect Molly from any more upset and was tempted to put away the photos of Molly with Sue to help her get over her sadness. However, with the support of her social worker, she kept talking to Molly about how much she must miss Sue and kept a special box of things she had brought with her from Sue's house in the living room, so Molly could take them out whenever she wanted to. Josie also put up a photograph taken of all of them during introductions to help Molly make sense of her story and the move from one family to another.

Sometimes it can be hard to accept the strength of feeling your child still has for their foster carer when you want them to form a relationship with you – but supporting them through grieving that relationship can help you form a closer bond over time. Some children take longer to work through these feelings and they might also experience sadness for other losses they have had – for family pets they left behind, favourite grandparents they no longer have contact with and for their birth parents they no longer live with – all this can become entangled in the immediate loss of their foster carer. Help them by showing that you are comfortable with talking about their loss – children may move in and out of feeling sad, but when they feel down, offering them comfort and accepting that they do feel so sad will help them work through these feelings and settle. Putting up a photograph in your home of your child with their foster carer and talking about them also gives your child the message that you can share their loss and understand how important this relationship was to them.

Creating a sense of safety

Now the challenge is to create a new family, understanding that your child may need support and a particular way of being a family, which recognises their history before they came to live with you. Creating a sense of safety for your child is the place to begin.

In her book *Nurturing Attachments*, Kim Golding outlines a model of parenting which focuses on creating a secure base as its foundation. She identifies how, for children who have experienced trauma and loss, a sense of safety is essential if they are to develop a more secure attachment relationship – your goal as an adoptive parent. Feeling safe, both physically and emotionally, forms the foundation for developing a secure attachment (Golding 2008).

To help your child feel safe in your family, first acknowledge that they may feel unsafe: 'it's scary to live in an new place,' but give them the message that they are safe with you – 'you are safe here and we will keep you safe.' Show you realise that they may not know or trust that this is the truth by talking about it. Some children need to see the physical evidence that your house is a safe one. If they have lived in a house where strange people turned up and came in, where things were taken and people were hurt, windows were broken and the police often came, then they will carry an anxiety about feeling unsafe in a house.

> Tom, aged six, moved to live with his adopters and struggled to settle at night. His adopters found out from his foster carer that she had also found him awake late at night, worried that something would happen. His birth family had been involved in drug-dealing and the neighbours had reported lots of fights and the police coming to the house late at night. Tom's adopters decided to take him round the house and show him that the front door was locked with a chain, the windows all had locks and that each night his parents would go round and check everything. With time he settled, but he continued to check his window lock every night before bed.

Making things routine and predictable

To help your child feel safe, a sense of predictability is essential, rather than living in a constant high alert as to what might happen next. Moving somewhere new provokes huge anxiety for children as they have no sense of what will happen and when. Imagine you are staying with someone on an exchange visit and you wake up on the first morning. You don't know what you will do that day, what to wear, what you will have for breakfast and you don't know the hosts well enough to ask them if you can call home. For your child, the first few weeks will mirror that sense of worry stemming from not knowing. To help them feel less confused and anxious, prepare them for what will happen – you might say: 'In the morning we do this …' or 'Our day looks like this.' Go through each part of the day, explaining who does what and when.

Spending the first weeks establishing a predictable, low-key routine will help your child gain a sense of security and stop them filling the unknown with worry.

Try using a whiteboard or stick-on pictures with velcro to help make a plan. Visual images can help children understand what is happening in a concrete way, which doesn't rely on their reading ability. They can help to draw or cut out the pictures and take part in sticking them on the plan to map out their day.

Laura adopted five-year-old Tyrone who had lived in a neglectful birth family before moving to a busy foster home. When he arrived he kept asking: 'Who is coming? Where are we going? What are we doing now?' To help build his sense of security and calm his anxiety, Laura made a chart for each day of the week and together they made a set of pictures to stick on for the day – plates to represent meals, boots for trips to the park, LEGO® for playtime, a bath and a bed for his night-time routine and a briefcase for social worker visits. Each day in the morning they stuck on the pictures for that day to help him develop a sense of how it would proceed.

Mapping out the week can help everyone feel safe. It can help you fill the week and feel more in control – it can feel strange adjusting to being at home if you have given up a busy full-time job. Putting together a plan can help with feeling at a bit of a loss if you are 'just' at home. Try to resist the temptation to fill the time with lots of outings – what your child needs is lots of at-home time, pottering about, allowing you to get to know each other. In contrast to having a biological family, which is a slow, organic process, your child has arrived in a matter of days so the process of getting to know each other needs to be your focus. This is best achieved at home, without distractions and other people. This can feel intense, but it is your chance to begin forging a deeper relationship with your child.

> Eve and Julian adopted George and Tim, two lively boys of two and four. When their social worker visited, they were feeling overwhelmed by the boys' demanding attention and Julian expressed a sense of not knowing what to do with them all the time. They put together a timetable for the week – marking every mealtime, bath and bedtime for each day, when they would go to the park to feed the ducks, when grandma was to visit and activities for each day as simple as going out for a welly walk or making chocolate cakes. Putting in everything that was to happen helped George and Tim develop a sense of how their family life was now – they had lived in a first home that was chaotic and they were often left hungry and dirty due to their birth mother's drug use. They needed this level of reassurance that they would get their needs met and be looked after. The high level of repetition in their plan also helped build their sense of safety through its familiarity – they began to expect that bath-time would follow teatime, whereas in their first home nothing was predictable and it was often a frightening place to be. Eve and Julian also talked to the boys about how they might be feeling – they wondered whether they were worried they might not have tea, or scared that Eve and Julian might leave in the night, as they had been abandoned by their

mum and left alone in the house. This helped them develop a sense of being safe and cared for. It also helped Eve and Julian to gain a sense of structure and purpose to their day as they had both been struggling with the transition from being at work all day to being at home full-time.

A sense of calm

Creating a calm atmosphere is key to creating a sense of safety – as is keeping out things that may trigger a sense of danger or conflict. Heather Moran (2010) suggests monitoring the television and radio to avoid exposing your child to stories of violence and trauma, which may trigger fear and difficult memories for them. Similarly, sit and watch their DVDs with them, as even fairy stories can be full of themes of loss and danger which might make them feel frightened – try Snow White, Hansel and Gretel or The Wizard of Oz for wicked parents, child-catchers and kidnapping. If you watch them together, you can share the experience, reassure them they are safe and consider their own story with them.

Staying calm as a parent is a major challenge for everyone – but particularly important when beginning to parent a child who has experienced trauma and not yet developed a secure attachment with you. Staying calm and empathic is key in facing any challenges your child may bring – from refusing to put their clothes on, to fighting with their sister. Rather than shouting at them to stop bickering and sending them to their rooms, you might say: 'Seems you two are finding it hard to play nicely this afternoon, let's all play a game together,' while keeping your tone soft and even. They may be challenging and protest at the responses you give them – but keeping calm and staying consistent helps to teach your child how difficulties are resolved in your family, without resorting to punishment or harsh criticism.

Your child may find this hard to get used to if they have lived in a very structured foster home where time-out was used as a frequent punishment, or if they have experienced harsh or neglectful parenting in their birth home – they will expect you to behave as all the other parents in their lives have behaved. They may escalate their behaviour just to see if you really can stay calm under pressure from them. Changing their expectations of you as a parent takes time and lots of repetition – you might need to say: 'I wonder if it feels strange, I know that your mum did it in a different way but in our family we do it this way.' They can then learn that you will parent them in a safe way.

Parenting to help your child thrive

When establishing a family life, which is attachment-friendly and helps your child feel safe, you need to take account of their early life experiences. They may behave with you just as they did with their birth parents or foster carers, in ways they have worked out to survive their family environment. They may behave as if they don't need you to look after them, or cling to you to make sure you don't abandon them. Mary Dozier (2003) describes the concept of therapeutic parenting as a way of changing the pattern – of challenging the way a child expects you to be with them and developing positive ways of relating with each other, rather than being fear-driven. In the early days of being together, you can model for the child how you are as a parent – one that does not harm them and meets their needs – over time they will have repeated experience of you as a safe parent and your relationship will grow with their trust in you.

Dan Hughes' model of parenting with PLACE (2009) offers a way to achieve this – he identifies five key elements which help you create a family life in which your child will feel secure and safe. He advocates parenting with:

- Playfulness – when there is spontaneous fun and enjoyment between you and your child and an element of lightness and hope in the relationship.

- Love – that you as the parent are motivated by your love and commitment to your child, and that what you do is because you have your child's best interests at heart.

- Acceptance – that you accept your child unconditionally, as worthwhile and worth loving. That does not mean that you accept any behaviour that you think is inappropriate, but that you can accept their motivation underlying the behaviour.

- Curiosity – that you as their parent are interested in their inner life, without judging them, but are keen to understand their thoughts, feelings and perceptions that led to a behaviour. You want to understand them better and that will help your child understand themselves more.

- Empathy – having empathy for your child means feeling their sadness and distress with them and having compassion for them. It enables your child to feel they can manage their experiences and not be overwhelmed by their feelings of anger or sadness as you will support them.

By using PLACE you will be able to connect with your child on an emotional level, which will help them to better understand their own emotional life and develop a sense of emotional safety with you as you show your understanding of their struggles (Hughes 2006). In the early days, playfulness will help you begin making a relationship with your child and maintaining empathy, curiosity and acceptance will engender a stronger connection between you. This can take a bit of practice when you are faced with an angry child who has just hit their brother, but when you approach the challenge of dealing with incidents like this using PLACE, you will begin to deepen the emotional connections between you that will enable your child to thrive.

The 'nos'

Parenting strategies you use need to be attachment-sensitive and acknowledge your child's early history. Avoid lots of shouting, sarcasm and harsh discipline – as well as smacking. Your child may have experienced these in their previous homes and they will confirm their self-image as unlovable and worthless. Smacking will model parenting that uses violence and may trigger memories of being hurt by their birth parents. However, all children need boundaries to develop into emotionally healthy adults who can live in a social world. They need discipline given in a calm and authoritative manner – you are modelling being a safe adult who is in charge of keeping them safe and who will teach them how to behave well. They need clear expectations of how you want them to behave and help to do this – they can't manage this on their own and they will resort to the strategies and behaviour they have used in the past. When they are naughty, they need a consequence so they can develop their sense of cause and effect and their social understanding. Any consequence needs to be developmentally appropriate, timely and make sense – and they need you to help them with it, rather than expect them to do it on their own. For example, if they have pulled the cat's tail, they need you to show them how to stroke the cat gently, and then to make amends by helping you to clean out the cat's food dish: if they have thrown their toys everywhere, they need to help tidy them away.

The word 'no' can trigger an extreme response – you may just say no to another biscuit and your child throws themselves on the floor and starts screaming. This word can trigger a sense of rejection and your child may react intensely – this will need exploring with them. They might feel rejected, but you can reassure them that you understand this is hard for them to manage – but they are still not getting another biscuit. Clarity and consistency are key – if you give in and change your mind in the face of a tantrum, they will feel confused and less safe; they need you to be in charge. Other children can be very controlling as they have learnt this keeps them safe; they need parenting which avoids direct confrontation to achieve the same outcome. Rather than telling them to put their shoes on, you could try racing them to put them on, or offer them either shoes or Wellingtons to put on. This gives them a sense of control over the choice they make, but they are still doing what you have asked them to do. Your tone of voice should stay light, with a sense of fun in racing them to be ready rather than getting cross and irritated. It takes a bit of practice to avoid getting into control-battles – and to remember why it is so important to your child to feel like they are in control. Learning which things need to be addressed and which things aren't worth having a big fight over also takes time – there may be something that drives you crazy whereas your partner can't understand why you are getting so irritated. It's worth exploring these issues to help you stay calm when you need to.

> Kate and Linda adopted Ben and Jack, twins aged four. After six weeks their social worker asked how things were going. Mealtimes were proving tricky and they reflected on their different approaches. Linda confessed that she was irritated by the boys eating so messily and didn't feel that Kate was backing her up in teaching them their table manners. Linda pointed out that given that the boys were only little and still getting used to being with them, keeping their mouths closed and sitting nicely seemed something to worry about later on. Kate acknowledged that in her own family good manners had been important to her mother and she had wanted her children to follow the same rules. They agreed to focus on helping the boys to enjoy sitting at the table with them for now.

Saying sorry

No one is perfect and everyone loses his or her temper sometimes – the critical thing is to repair the break in your relationship if you get cross and shout or say something that you wish you hadn't. Reflect on your child's experience of other adults getting cross with them – they may have shouted right in their face, been moody with them for days or sent them to their room. If you lose your temper, you need to apologise and repair your relationship as soon as you are calm enough to do so. An 'I'm sorry' and a hug works better than a lengthy explanation of why you got angry. Acknowledging that it may have made them feel scared or worried, or reminded them of other times, can help your child make sense of their feelings and reassure them that in this relationship you will make sure they are safe.

If your child does something wrong and is told off, they may experience a sense of shame. When a child does something wrong when they are little, they experience a sense of shame and a break in their relationship with their parent. For example, if they throw a toy at the dog, their parent might say 'no' sharply and have a cross face, and they may burst into tears, feeling bad. In a secure relationship their parent will comfort them, talk about what was wrong and help them learn the consequences of their actions. The child will learn that it was not them but what they did that the parent is unhappy with. Over time they will learn to feel guilt for something that they have done wrong, know that they can say sorry and that their relationship can be restored with their parent. But when a child is left feeling shame, they struggle to acknowledge what they have done, feel angry and blame other people. When their parent does not repair their relationship, the child is left feeling that they are a bad person because of what they did. A child that has experienced trauma is frequently triggered into shame and needs empathy with their overwhelming sense that they are a bad person – they need to learn that it is the behaviour you are not happy with, not them as a person (Golding and Hughes 2012).

If your child does something wrong, consider how you are going to respond. A previous foster carer or birth parent may have sent them to their room as punishment, or made them sit on the stairs in time-out. For a child who does not have a secure attachment relationship or who has experienced abuse and neglect, being sent away can feel like being rejected and abandoned all over again. Their bedroom should be a safe place for sleeping and playing, not a place for punishment.

It is unhelpful to send your child away when they are still in the process of making a relationship with you. Keeping them close and helping them calm down if they have become upset or angry will help them learn that you will help them stay safe and calm and that you can manage any big feelings that they have. Sometimes having a quiet space where you can both 'sit and think about it' helps, or try taking them away from the rest of the family into the kitchen and pottering around while they calm down, talking all the while in a gentle, singsong voice. This will help regulate them and reassure them that you are still there and not going anywhere, even when they are angry. Get them to help you make a den in the kitchen or living room, so they have a quiet, safe space they can use to calm down in but still stay near you rather than being sent away. They will learn to manage their feelings through repeated experiences of you managing these feelings for them. You play a key role in helping them learn new ways of expressing their feelings through how you parent them.

Being independent

Your child may be self-reliant and want to do everything for themselves. This could be because no one in their birth family looked after them, so they had to look after themselves – and this can sometimes have been reinforced by foster carers who focused on developing their independence. Your child might, at the age of three, be dressing themselves, brushing their own teeth and generally able to care for themselves because they have had to. They may resist you trying to look after them. They may look to their sibling to care for them because that was their role in their birth family – an older sibling may feel they have to look after their younger brother or sister, wanting to feed and change them and seeing it as their role not yours. Their survival in their birth home may have depended on this and it can be hard for them to give up this role. In a new family, this parental role can be triggered for older siblings as they feel heightened anxiety. They will need patient support to relinquish this role as it links to their sense of responsibility for the survival of their younger siblings.

> Kelly, aged seven, and Joanne, aged two, arrived at Peter and Sue's house clutching each other's hands. During the first few weeks, Kelly struggled to settle and kept running to check on Joanne's whereabouts. She got very cross when Sue insisted that Joanne hold her hand and not Kelly's to cross the road. She also kept wanting to change Joanne's nappy, despite Sue explaining she didn't have to. Sue gently told Kelly that she was the mummy and that she would take care of both of them – she understood that when Kelly was little her birth mother often went out, so Kelly had to take care of Joanne but she didn't need to do this anymore. Over time Kelly's anxiety lessened and she gave up her sense of parenting responsibility for her little sister – although when they went to the park, she still worried about where Joanne was.

As you begin to parent your child, you may initially be impressed by the things they can do for themselves and which may have been strongly encouraged by their foster carer. But for your child to develop a secure attachment with you, they need to experience being cared for in a way which meets their needs as a much younger child. This will start to make up for the care they may have lacked. You need to encourage their dependence on you as their parent, so they can experience you as the kind of parent who they can trust to meet their needs. Parent them with a high level of supervision and don't give them the opportunity to do too much by themselves – as with toddlers, stay close by all the time so you can keep an eye on them and be present with them. Take any opportunity for close physical care and play so they can experience you as a nurturing parent. They may suddenly ask you to put their socks on for them, even though they can dress themselves: see this as an opportunity, not a chore. They may begin to ask to be looked after as if they were younger than they actually are; they may ask to be picked up and carried, they may ask to be fed or to drink from a bottle.

Sometimes this makes adopters feel uncomfortable as it conflicts with their ideas about encouraging children to grow up and be independent. But meeting their need to be little will help them to grow emotionally once the gaps have been filled.

> Annie and Steve adopted Joseph aged seven, who had come into care aged five. He had lived with his birth mother who was an alcoholic and Joseph had to take care of himself a lot of the time. When Joseph arrived, he seemed very grown-up and Annie described it as like having a lodger in the house, he didn't seem to need them at all.
>
> They worked hard over the first few months to try to take care of him – they made time to play games with him and at bath-time made a point of giving him a special play time with bubbles and then read him a story, even though he kept saying he could read to himself. When he bumped his knee and did not make a fuss they noticed he had hurt himself and offered him a cuddle and some special cream to make it better. They talked with him about his story and how, when he was very little, his birth mother had not been able to look after him, so he had had to take care of himself. They explained that now they wanted to take care of him, as his mum and dad. Gradually Joseph began to let them do more and more for him, and he started to curl up on Annie's lap in front of the television like a baby. She would wrap him in a blanket and rock him as she would have done if she had been his mummy when he was little and needed taking care of.

Helping your child feel calm and emotionally regulated

As a baby your child may have been left to cry – no one may have picked them up, rocked them, soothed them and found out why they were crying, whether they were wet, hungry, bored or lonely. They may have been left unhappy, cross and uncomfortable, when what they needed was an adult who was loving and responsive and who recognised their cry as a state of distress. They needed an adult who, on discovering this distress, was moved to find the source – maybe hunger, pain or tiredness – and then to meet that need, providing calming reassurance and restoring a sense of emotional security and peace again, a process called co-regulation. Through this ongoing, daily co-regulation, a child learns to feel secure in their care-givers and in themselves. They learn that their needs can be met and their voice heard. Over time, a child learns to recognise and then regulate their own emotional and physical states (Golding 2008, Bhreathnach 2009). Without this repeated experience, a child struggles to regulate their own emotions as they grow up. They can become quickly upset, cross or overexcited and struggle to calm down again. Even the tiniest thing can seem to send them over the edge. What they need is the experience of an adult helping them to recognise what they are feeling and how to calm themselves again. This will be your role as your child's new parent as you help your child to recognise their feelings and learn how to manage them.

You may notice in the first few weeks that your child might become overexcited at the prospect of a trip out or very restless or easily upset when playing with their brother or sister and then find it hard to calm down again – they are struggling to regulate their emotional states. You can help them regulate their feelings by doing it with them. Notice how they are feeling and help them to feel calmer, less angry, less upset and less uncomfortable. Talking with them about these feelings helps: 'It seems you are finding it really hard to sit and wait for grandma to come, why don't you come and sit with me and we will read a book together until she arrives?', or, 'You seem to be struggling to play with Ben and getting cross with the game – shall I play out in the garden with you both for a while?' You then recognise their feelings, and acknowledge that they are finding things hard, while helping them to feel calmer.

Your child's early experiences of trauma, neglect and disrupted attachments will mean they will revert to survival behaviours to stay safe. You may notice that these behaviours are triggered on moving in with you as the new experience makes them feel unsafe. You may notice the fight, flight or freeze response as discussed earlier – either pattern may predominate or they may present a different response to a different situation. You might notice that when the social worker comes to visit, your child may become very still and not move – and you may notice that when you take them to the supermarket they run off and hide – using different survival behaviours in different environments. Over time these will become clearer to you – but they may be immediately obvious, too. Dan Hughes has described these responses as hit, run or hide and it's helpful to remember this as you try to understand what is going on for your child.

> Ellie, aged four, had been living with her adopters Gary and Martin and her brother Sam, aged three, for four weeks when their social worker came to visit, bringing the reviewing officer who had been overseeing their case since Ellie and Sam had come into care two years previously. The children had been playing together in the living room, but as soon as the two social workers walked in, a fight started over the toy train. Ellie did not respond to Martin's request to stop hitting her brother but ran upstairs and hid under her bed. Only with much persuasion did she come back downstairs and sit on Martin's lap while the social workers explained that they had come just to visit and she was not going anywhere. Ellie had been triggered into her survival state and 'hit, run, hide' response by the arrival of two people who reminded her of her scary past.

If your child is triggered into one of these responses, they need your help to feel calm and safe again. Your challenge is to change their established patterns by offering them a safe and predictable family life with repeated experiences that will alter the way they respond to stress (Perry 2006; Hughes 2013).

In helping children to feel more emotionally regulated and calm, also consider their sensory responses to the world around them. If they have experienced a high level of early neglect and poor early attachments, they may have problems with sensory integration and regulation. Spend some time noticing how they respond to different sensory experiences and whether they struggle to regulate their response. These experiences could be related to taste, sight, smell, sound, touch, movement or body positioning and force or pressure. They may respond to sensory experiences by becoming cut off or even shut down – or they may respond by becoming agitated, aggressive or overexcited and need calming, suggesting that the sensation is either in itself overwhelming and they have become overstimulated by it or that it triggers an emotional memory that is painful for them. Their response will depend on their past emotional and sensory experiences, and their capacity for regulation. Their response to particular noises, smells or touches may surprise you but remember that they may be responding to sensations in a way that is shaped by their past. They might need help to achieve a calm, regulated state and you can support them with this. Be aware of all the different sensory experiences in their environment and offer them ones that help them to remain in an appropriate calm-alert state for the situation they are in. Use all the different senses including smells, sounds, tastes, and the feel of things, as well as movement. Notice how they respond, because on different days and in different emotional states they may respond differently and what one child likes another may not. Children who have experienced neglect may need to be carefully introduced to different sensory experiences to help them develop better sensory integration. You can offer them a nurturing sensory environment which will help them better understand the messages their senses are giving them and enable them to respond appropriately to them and use them as a means to regulate themselves when they are in a state of distress.

For children that need alerting, try activities such as jumping on a trampoline or quick swinging and rocking in a chair, eating crunchy food such as carrot sticks or crisps, blowing bubbles or whistles, playing cotton-ball football with straws, dancing or playing with fidget toys such as Koosh Balls. For children that need calming, try activities such as slow swinging or rocking, listening to classical music or natural sounds like water, squeezing stress balls or putty, using a heavy blanket on their bed, eating chewy food such as toffee or toast, having a warm drink or having a quiet space such as a tent with blankets and cushions (Laurie 2013; Scully 2013). Each child is different so you have to see what suits your child and notice how they respond to what you offer them. Giving them different sensory experiences can help them feel more regulated, which also supports their attachment relationship with you, as you are able to build a closer connection. Using positive sensory experiences will create a sense of nurture and safety as well as support their developing better sensory integration (Ayres 1991; Bhreathnach 2009; Laurie 2013).

> Karen had adopted Jade, aged five. Jade had experienced extreme neglect and chaos when she lived with her birth parents for the first three years of her life. When Jade started school, she really struggled with the separation from Karen and would come home in a really agitated, grumpy state so their evenings did not go well. To help Jade with her anxiety when she came home, Karen started using some regulating sensory strategies to help her feel calmer. On the way home in the car, she gave her a tangle toy to play with and a drink with a sports-lid so she had to suck at it which helped regulate her. Once they were home, Karen made her a plate of toast and jam to eat and a hot chocolate in her special cup. Then they would snuggle up together under a soft blanket to watch children's television together. The warm, chewy toast with the jam and salty butter was a calming and nurturing snack, so Jade was able to feel calmer and soothed, having struggled through the school day. At bath-time, Karen ran her a bath with sweet-smelling bubbles and then wrapped her up in a soft, warm towel before putting on her warm pyjamas and tucking her into her bed. All these calming and nurturing sensory experiences soothed Jade and calmed her as she developed her relationship with Karen.

Tasha and Dave had just adopted Toby, aged six, and Carys, aged four, and were finding it hard to manage car journeys, as the children would fight and cry as soon as they set off. Both Toby and Carys had had twice-weekly contact with their birth mother and three older siblings while in foster care. The contact had been chaotic, with lots of shouting and squabbling between the children. Tasha and Dave chose some regulating strategies to try and stop every car journey being so stressful. They bought both children a soft blanket to tuck round them and a tiny fluffy toy to hold. As they set off, Tasha would give them each a drink in a sippy cup and a chewy fruit-stick to eat. She put on some nursery rhymes and they sang as they drove. Both children were soothed and calmed by these strategies and their distress lessened. Over time they developed a different response to car journeys as their experience of them became less triggering and they were less disregulated by the start of the engine.

The same principles apply to grown ups – using similar strategies to help you feel calmer and more regulated will help you parent more successfully. Take some time to work out your own patterns of behaviour when you are stressed and what happens when you become disregulated. Once you can recognise your own patterns of behaviour, you can use regulating strategies to help you feel calmer and less stressed as and when you need to. Reflecting on how you respond when you are stressed, upset or angry and what helps you calm down can be helpful preparation for when things are tricky in the first few weeks (Bhreathnach 2009; Scully 2013).

Amanda adopted a little girl, Becky, aged three. By the end of the first week she began to see that tea time was a struggle for both of them – Becky did not want to sit at the table and eat and Amanda could feel herself getting wound up by Becky's refusal to eat her tea and she started to get impatient with Becky. When she felt herself getting cross, she decided to get up to put the kettle on and made herself a calming cup of tea. Once Becky was in bed, Amanda ran herself a hot bath, full of bubbles and lit a scented candle to help her relax and calm down after a stressful day. Using these strategies helped her to regulate herself and keep a positive connection with her daughter.

Playful parenting

Alongside regulating activities, play can help you begin to create positive attachment relationships in the early days. You can use play in all sorts of ways to help build your relationship – play can help you find out how your child feels, give you a sense of their inner world and help build and strengthen their attachment with you (Golding and Hughes 2012). It is also the way to bring a sense of fun into your family – something that can get lost in all the anxiety and pressure of introductions. Given that your child may not have experienced secure attachments and not had their needs met when young, they may struggle to play and need your help. Sometimes children find it hard to relax and play as they are scared and hypervigilant. As they are on the alert for bad things to happen and constantly watchful to protect themselves, play is hard for them to engage in. If they have become self-reliant they may find it hard to play with others, as they tend to avoid intimacy. Children who are very controlling struggle to play successfully with others as they find it hard to share or take turns being in charge. Children who are very anxious can't play alone as they are afraid of being abandoned. If they are easily triggered into their survival behaviours, they may struggle to be calm and to manage their emotions and interactions with others. If they have been neglected, they may just not know how to play.

Play helps create attachments in a fun and creative way – developing trust through repeated playtimes. Your child will experience you as safe, trustworthy and attuned to them. This will support their recovery from the impact of the trauma they have experienced (Perry 2010). Your child will probably be functioning at a much younger emotional age than their chronological age, so it is important to offer play experiences to match their emotional level. Spending time playing toddler and baby games gives your child the chance to experience interactions they may have missed or been too scared to engage with – and this also helps them grow emotionally. Playing younger games also gives children the experience of being successful, rather than being frustrated or feeling a failure. Start with DUPLO, rather than LEGO. Don't push them to play with age-appropriate toys, as they need to make up for the play they have missed first. Source toys from friends or car-boot sales so they can play with them and then move on to the next level without any pressure to feel you have got your money's worth from expensive, new toys.

Your child may not have had the opportunity to have lots of sensory play, even though this is an essential part of their development. It gives them the chance to experiment with how things feel and allows them to feel in a safe and fun way. For example, try:

- playing in a sandpit and paddling pool, use lots of cups and buckets for digging and pouring

- playing in the bath with cups, boats and bubbles

- Play-Doh and clay

- finger and face painting.

Give your child the chance to get messy and wet, to take their shoes and socks off and explore. Set up some boundaries around this play to start teaching them about safe limits and show that the grown-up is in charge. This may not have been their experience in the past. They may have been left to play without any adults keeping an eye on where all the water went or making sure that they did not throw sand in each other's faces. Watch their reaction to this kind of play – children who have been very compliant and reserved to keep safe may struggle with being messy and can only tolerate it in very small doses, while others who feel empty because their needs have not been met, can want more and more and more and find it hard to tolerate being set any limits on how much they paint they use or how much water they pour and where.

Cooking is another good way to introduce children to sensory play – stick to simple ideas – and cooking involves all the senses, as well as being interactive. Cooking also shows that the adult in charge will keep them safe, and that the adult sets the limits – so only you will open the hot oven and only you will decide how many cookies they can eat when they are ready. One adoptive mum confessed to being no good at cooking, but she started using packet mixes with great results – her daughter loved the time they spent together stirring and icing and the whole family enjoyed the cakes.

For play to build attachments it needs to be interactive – build in times when you play together rather than your child playing alone while you potter or read the newspaper. Focus less on educating and more on deepening your relationship through play. Avoid letting your child spend too much time on a games console or watching the television – they have a place for quiet time and for relaxing, but too much can lead to disturbed sleep patterns, high levels of arousal and detachment from interaction with the family.

Aaron had just started school and his mum, Cath, noticed that after school he sat in front of the computer and would not budge, despite the best efforts of his brother to get him to play. Aaron seemed to disappear into his own world and did not answer if Cath called him – if she switched the computer off, he erupted with temper. Aaron had spent two years living in a home where both adults fought constantly – his survival strategy was to cut off from all the violence and noise around him by losing himself in the computer game. Cath began to sit next to him and watch with him, talking about what they were doing. After half an hour she would give him a warning that it was nearly time to come off, they would then have a snack and go and play outside with his brother. In their house, she wanted him to learn that he did not need to use his survival strategy as he was safe and did not need to switch off from the world.

Children who have experienced neglect and loss can find it hard to play by themselves. They can feel abandoned or rejected if told to go off and play. They benefit from much more adult-led play than you would expect for a child of their age. Once they have developed a more secure relationship with you, they will be more able to play independently. Other children who may have been left alone for long periods of time or have been lost in a very busy household may have developed a more self-reliant pattern of playing by themselves. These children might need more encouragement to play with you. They may find the experience of an adult wanting to give them their full attention uncomfortable and surprising – so they may resort to their familiar pattern of doing things by themselves. Go slowly and play little and often if they are struggling to engage with you – catch them by surprise with a game of hide-and-seek or play with their favourite cars. If they find it hard to play then notice this and come back to play again together later on.

Games to try:

- blow bubbles together and pop them

- 'Row, row the boat'

- 'Round-and-round the garden'

- 'This little piggy went to market'

- 'hide-and-seek' and 'peekaboo'

- 'pat-a-cake'

- thumb-wrestling

- singing songs with actions – 'Wheels on the bus', 'Rock a bye baby'.

All these kinds of games include elements of rhythmic play, eye contact, safe touch, sensory play and interaction between you – all essential parts of building positive attachments. Lots of nursery games and songs mirror these elements and you can play games you used to play when you were young or that your older children have enjoyed before. As researchers have commented, when considering helping children to develop positive neural connections, these kinds of interactions, which are repeated, rhythmical and interactive, are critical to helping them heal (Cohen 2001; Perry 2010; Jernberg and Booth 2010).

Story-time is a lovely opportunity for building your relationship – your child may not have had the experience of an adult making the time to sit with them and share stories, and it is a good way to enable them to experience you as attuned and focused on them in a playful and nurturing way. You can read together, make up stories with dolls, puppets and toys or play dress-up. Story-time can offer your child the chance to explore their experiences or things that may worry them in a safe way, as well as being time to enjoy closeness and nurture, cuddled up next to you with a good story. There are suggestions for stories about particular issues in the 'Books for Children' section at the back of this book; reading about themes they can identify with can help support your child with any difficult experiences they have had – but regular story-time with you is in itself a really positive thing for your child.

Play-fighting or wrestling can be great fun and encourage positive physical activity and connection, but this needs safe limits set by you as the adult. Introduce a 'no hurting rule' and rituals around the game to give it a safe structure. Children need to be able to calm down and manage the excitement to be able to play safely.

Alex and Ben loved to wrestle their dad and kept jumping on him to start a game, which made him cross when they

caught him by surprise. The game would often end in tears
with one of them getting hurt. They worked out a plan for
the game, setting out their rules – on starting they would
bow to each other, then wrestle for three bouts and at the
end they would bow and make the sound of a bell ringing
to signal the time to stop. This proved more successful and
stopped things getting out of hand.

Some children may struggle with the limits set for them if they
have lived in a chaotic house. For other children, play-fighting
may trigger traumatic memories of living with domestic violence
or in a family where there was lots of fighting – they may become
aggressive and struggle to calm down. If this happens, it may be
best not to play these kinds of games until they are more able
to regulate their responses. Play-fighting at bedtime is also best
avoided if you want your child to calm down enough to sleep
(Cohen 2001).

If you adopt siblings, their experience of play will include
elements of rivalry and competition which may escalate without
adult supervision. They may bring with them patterns of playing
which were created in their birth family – you may see one sibling
try to control the play of another, one may always want what the
other one has or may ruin their game rather than join in, they
may be unable to sort out their differences other than by fighting
or by one always giving in to the other. While all siblings will
have some of these struggles, their ability to resolve differences
or feel safe with each other will have been compromised by
their experience of neglectful parenting. If their parents did not
teach them how to share, how to play or how to sort things out
without hurting each other, they will have developed their own
strategies and ways of interacting based on their experience of
conflict and a struggle to get their needs met. Children may also
act out their early traumatic experiences with each other; these
are triggered just by being together as they share a common
history of neglect, violence and fear. If this is the case, you will
need to give your children a much higher level of supervision

and be much more involved in their play to help them learn to play safely and well together.

It helps build their attachment relationship with you if you can give each child some time alone with you, as well as time with their brothers and sisters to play as a family. Enlist grandparents or aunts and uncles to help support you if you have a large family. Older children often value having a slightly later bedtime so they can play a quiet game with you or watch a special programme together when their younger sibling is in bed – if they are at school, they often feel they are missing out on time with you while the younger one is getting all your attention so noticing this can help. Use structured family games to help them learn to play together, take turns and to win and lose without having a fall-out or resorting to cheating. They need adults to demonstrate play without shouting, tantrums or fighting to resolve their differences. If board games are too hard, go back to the games you play with much younger children – building brick towers, playing with racing cars and pushing doll prams around to create repeated times of having fun together where they have you as the adult giving them safety through supervision and giving the play structure and limits.

Children who are controlling can struggle with play and can become competitive and bossy – they may find it hard to play with other children and may need additional support from you and the teachers at school to learn how to play well with their peers. If they have a friend over to play, you may need to plan the play-date with a high level of structure to help it to go well – just telling them to go off and play can mean they either fall out or play separately and then their friend becomes bored and would rather go home. Short, structured play-dates with one other child can be more helpful in building their friendships.

When you are new to playful parenting you may encounter some challenges:

Your child may say everything is boring; they may be anxious about what or how to play. Don't take it personally, but offer them more support to start to play.

Your child may always want to be in charge, which can be wearing for you or their brother or sister; this may be their survival strategy. They need help to feel safe enough to let other people take a turn at choosing what they play and you can practise games with them that involve taking turns, or try some adult-led play for them to experience you as the one in charge, who also keeps them safe.

Your child might struggle to stop playing and refuse to get ready to go and pick up their sibling from school or do something else. The experience of something ending may trigger worries about separation and loss. They need help with managing to move from one activity to the next and you can assist by giving them time-warnings and planning with them.

Some children struggle to focus and hop from one thing to another with you following them – they may start something, be distracted or decide something else looks more interesting and never really settle to one game. They may feel anxious or be experiencing a high level of arousal, they may be hypervigilant to signs of threat or find it hard to choose and then not like what they have chosen. They may need help to feel calmer and less disregulated before they can settle to play. They may need more adult-led play on a one-to-one basis to help them focus and fewer choices to make choosing easier. Playtime is one of the most valuable experiences you can enjoy with your child and a great way to start building your relationships.

CHAPTER EIGHT

● ● ● ● ● ● ● ● ● ● ●

Challenges and How to Meet Them

When first at home, your child may respond to things you do or say in ways that puzzle you and may behave in ways that surprise or worry you. Try to think about these responses from an attachment and trauma perspective. This will help you decide whether these responses could be connected to their early experiences. Sometimes people explain difficulties as they are 'just being four' or he is 'just being a typical boy' or even that the children have had 'too much sugar'. Using the attachment and trauma framework of ideas will help you understand their responses and give you ideas as to how best to meet these challenges.

Trauma triggers

Neglect or frightening experiences when very young affect how a child functions as they grow. Their brain processes information using a template formed when they were very young – they expect people to behave and events to unfold according to this pre-existing template. The triggers which cause their brain to process things as dangerous may not be obvious to you – you have a different template for how the world works. Understanding what has activated your child's survival strategies can be crucial in helping them feel safe. In the early days, certain things might send your child into a survival state – they may be triggered into a fight, flight or freeze response by situations or people. Being aware of these can help you support them and help them to begin to create a different template for how the world works.

Sudden events

A stable routine and a predictable day create a sense of safety. Focus on this in the early days. Sometimes things crop up and plans need to change – an emergency trip to the dentist for you or maybe a school meeting you have to go to with their sibling. This can trigger a sense of fear in them, as their world is suddenly unpredictable again. Talking to your child about the need to change plans and acknowledging that they may feel disappointed and worried can help them to manage this. Use a timetable to show them that, after the change, there will be a return to the things you had planned together. If you have to leave them, understand that they may worry if someone is coming to look after them, even if they have already met this person. Give them something of yours to look after and hold onto, such as a scarf with your scent on it or a key-ring with your photo in it, even a special pen you have in your pocket – the message is that you will be returning to them and they can give it back to you then. Remember that lots of people may have looked after them before and some of them they have never seen again – your leaving suddenly, even for a short while, can trigger a strong sense of abandonment again.

In the second week of Kelly living with Janet and Jo, Janet got a call from her older daughter Beth's school – Beth had fallen and needed to go to hospital. Janet asked her mum to come round and then sat down with Kelly on the sofa: 'I've got to take Beth to the doctor, so Gran will stay with you until I get back. Gran will make you a sandwich and then you will watch Cinderella and play with your doll. You might feel worried, but Gran will stay all the time until I am back. I am going to give you my special hanky to put in your pocket so you can hold it if you feel worried.' Janet knew that Kelly had often been left alone in the house while her birth mother went out. When the police found Kelly, she had been wandering on the road looking for food so Janet felt it was important to stress that Kelly would not be hungry and would not be alone while Janet went to collect her sister.

Sudden departures can trigger anxiety, but your child may also struggle when you go out on a planned trip without them. They can become very clingy or grumpy and you may be tempted to cancel your trip and stay with them. But after living with you for a while (how long depends on each child), they will be secure enough to learn to manage the separation. They may need lots of reassurance and their other parent there to support them, but this is a critical part of their new template of the world.

You can say to them: 'You might be worried that I am not coming back, but I am going out to the gym for an hour and then I will come and say goodnight when I am home again.' They need to learn that although you go out and leave them, you also come back – in contrast to other adults that they have experienced going out and not returning, or returning drunk, high or too tired to notice that they were hungry, needed changing or soothing.

Visitors

Just as your leaving can trigger anxiety, so can visitors coming to your house. This might trigger memories of living in a house where lots of people came and went – and where the children were exposed to adults in an unsafe way. They might worry that a new person who you welcome in might hurt them or take them away. Visitors may bring on survival behaviour, as your child struggles to feel safe. Your child might suddenly become awkward and antagonistic, just when you want them to impress. They may become extremely charming and climb up on the visitor's lap, totally ignoring you. They may insist on the visitor's full attention, wanting them to play with them and them only, wanting them to come up to their bedroom and monopolising their time.

Try to prepare your child for who is coming, when and why – reassure them that the visitors are friends of yours and that you will keep your child safe. Planning the visit and explaining what you will do can also help – describe where you will sit, when you will make a cup of tea and how they can help with the cakes. Talk about how spending time in your house with strangers might make them feel a bit uncertain – be clear that if they need a cuddle or the loo or anything else, they should come to you. Preparing your visitors also helps – ask them to be mindful of their possible impact on your child and explain that you are all learning to be a family. Request that if your child tries to sit on their lap or asks them for a biscuit, they redirect them to you.

Social workers doing their statutory visits can raise even greater alarm – they may represent a connection with the birth family if they have been involved for a long time. The social worker's visit and their bag may represent another move or remind them of when they came into care. Sometimes social workers are given a rapturous and affectionate welcome when they arrive. You may feel rejected by this apparently preferential treatment for the social worker – it may be the pull of someone familiar reappearing or a behaviour to manage their sense of anxiety. Social workers who are sensitive to this can help by prompting your child to return to you.

Sophie had been living with Beth for six weeks when her social worker, Julie, came for a review and brought her manager with her. Sophie went straight up to Julie's manager with a big smile and asked her if she would like to see her bedroom. Julie intervened and suggested they ask Sophie's mummy if they could all see her new room together, as Sophie had not met her manager before. Sophie's survival strategy of pleasing strangers and going to anyone had been triggered by the arrival of someone linked to her frightening past.

Car journeys

Your child may have had difficult experiences linked to being in the car. They may have been removed from their birth family by car, sometimes in a police car, sitting in the back without a known adult with them. They may have journeyed back and forth to contact visits in a taxi or in the foster carers' car, but been left at contact without their safe adult with them. Even tiny babies may have travelled several times a week to have contact with their birth parents – this may have disrupted their routines, sleep patterns and sense of safety. When looking at their life-story book, children often point out their driver and escort as significant people in their lives as they have spent so much time with them going back and forth between foster homes, school and contact visits. Some contact visits will have been difficult, with siblings fighting and birth parents arguing. One foster carer described how the baby she was caring for always came back smelling of smoke from the birth father's clothes. The baby was then hard to settle, wouldn't take her bottle and every time the taxi came, she started to grizzle as she was put in the car. If birth parents have put their child into the car and have become distressed saying goodbye while they do their child's belt up, the sensory experience of being belted up and the engine starting can be enough to trigger strong memories of these past experiences. As these experiences are sensory, the child is often unable to articulate why they feel so distressed.

You may find that your child is reluctant to get in the car or is unhappy as you travel. They may take this out on their sibling if they are next to them in the car and may fight or try to get out of their car seat – all these are responses to the sensory memories they are experiencing. Other children fall straight to sleep when they get in the car as a 'shut out' survival strategy – rather than fight or flight, they freeze to manage their anxiety. They have a template of journeys leading to stressful situations and uncertainty about where they will go. To start with, try to avoid long car journeys and rehearse short journeys, to the shops and back, or to grandma's and back, to encourage them to develop a new positive template of journeys which always ends with them coming home. Sensory strategies to help them feel safe and calm can help regulate their emotions if they are struggling with car journeys. Offering them something sweet to chew, something soft to hold and playing music to sing along to can all help.

> Davey, aged three, would roar every time his mum put him in his car seat, and would make a huge fuss all the way to nursery. She sensed that the impending separation from her was the reason for his reaction and she tried talking to him about what would happen after nursery, repeating that then they would go home together. She gave him a bear to hold and he would sit in the car seat chewing at its ear – this helped regulate his anxiety and manage the journey better. Over time his anxiety lessened.

Trips away

Staying home and not going far before returning helps build a sense of security. After a while a trip away with friends and their children can seem a good idea, but for a child who has experienced many moves and whose new attachment relationships are still fragile, going away can be very frightening. They may not have had time to develop a sense of certainty in their new life – suitcases and a different environment with new sensory experiences can trigger anxiety that they are going to move again.

> Deidre and Sam had always planned to take their children camping, so when the summer came they bought a tent and had a successful practice overnight in the garden with their twins, Jenny and Julie. Feeling confident they packed for a trip to the seaside; they were excited to take the girls somewhere new. However, for most of the week neither girl seemed to relax, they kept squabbling and wandering off round the campsite with anyone they met. By the end of the week, Deidre and Sam were exhausted and happy to pack up and go home – but neither Jenny nor Julie could be persuaded to help put the things in the car. Just as they were about to leave, the girls refused to get in the car, demanding ice-creams before they left. After a showdown in the middle of the campsite, Sam hit the nail on the head – she asked the girls if they thought they weren't going home with them and they nodded. Despite the practice run, which had been on familiar home-ground, they had not felt secure enough for such a big trip away so soon.

To allay anxiety about any trip, give your child an idea of where they will be staying, what the place will look like and who they will meet. Take their pillows and any special toys and let them sleep in their sleeping-bags at home before you go, so they smell and feel familiar once away. The most important thing your child needs is to know that you will all be coming back together – so planning and outlining what you will do as a family when you get home is essential. Perhaps they can invite their grandparents to tea on the weekend they get back, or make a thank-you card to give to the neighbours who fed the cat while they were away.

Bedtime

This can be a tricky part of the day when you are all tired. Your child's early experiences may make this time even more challenging. In their birth family, they may not have had a regular bedtime or even a sense of night and day, as in some homes the curtains are never opened and if a light bulb blows it is not replaced so the house is often dark. Your child may not have been put to bed or had a bed with clean covers; they may have been left to sleep in their pushchair or on the sofa. They may have been hungry or thirsty, cold or dirty so it would have been hard to go to sleep and if they cried no one may have come to soothe them. In their birth family they may have heard or seen inappropriate adult activity at night and may have been vulnerable to abuse in their bedroom. While in foster care they may not have had a story, but a strict routine with the light out and door shut at bedtime, with older foster children still downstairs.

Coming to live in a new home where they are not sure about what will happen can make them anxious about going to sleep – their early sleep experience may disrupt their attempts to sleep in a new family home. Some children will have learnt a sleep pattern in their foster home, which they will bring into your home. They may settle quickly and sleep through the night, so sticking to the foster carer's routine will help. Others may find it harder to settle – they may struggle to go to sleep, may cry and demand that you stay, they may settle initially but then keep coming back downstairs or they may use delaying tactics, asking for one more story or one more biscuit before they go to bed. Other children may wake in the night and want to sleep in your bed, or they may have nightmares or bad dreams and call out.

If your child does not settle well, it may make you tired and stressed; broken nights leave everyone feeling exhausted and it is easy to lose your empathy for your child. Rather than seeing their struggles as naughty or manipulative, try to remember the underlying fear that they are battling and their need for comfort. Caroline Archer has described going to sleep as letting go of your watch on the world – if you don't feel safe or can't predict what will happen when you close your eyes and sleep, then staying awake is the only way to protect yourself (Archer 2012).

A foster carer has described a little girl coming to stay after her removal from her birth family late at night after a drug raid. She was two years old, exhausted and sat upright on the carer's lap. She started to nod off, but every time her head dropped she would jerk herself back up and open her eyes again – she could not let herself sleep as she did not feel safe.

To create a sense of safety at sleep time, your child needs a calm and predictable bedtime routine. Use sensory strategies to help soothe and calm them and let them know that you will be there to keep them safe. Keeping to roughly the same bedtime every night helps, even at the weekends and in the holidays. This may seem onerous but will help them sleep better. Use a routine of play, bath, story and snack or bottle in a predictable order that suits you and teaches them how bedtime will go in your family. Sensory strategies are helpful to soothe their nervous system. A snack and a warm milk drink will help them feel full and calm. Hang their pyjamas and towel over the radiator so they are warm after their bath. Read them a story, sing them a lullaby and leave a night light on once you leave the room. Some children feel calmer when they have a heavy blanket on their bed and others like to be tucked in tight – experiment to see what suits your child (Bhreathnach 2012). Having slept on your sheets and pillowcases at the foster carer's and then transferred them to your house, the smell and feel of these will be familiar. Put a large photo of you by their bed to give them a reassuring image next to them. A cuddly toy or special blanket to hold can be calming, but try not to wash it too often as it will lose its comforting smell if it's too clean. Some adopters read stories onto MP3 players, tablets or discs, so their child can listen to their voice to soothe them. Leave the light on in the hallway and the door ajar – particularly for those children who were shut in their rooms in previous homes.

Ella moved to her adoptive mum and dad's house on the edge of a small village. After several weeks she was still struggling to settle at night, despite the foster carer's report that she always settled quickly and slept right through. They considered what had changed for Ella to try and work out how to help her sleep. She had lived with her siblings in a busy foster home and was now the only child in the house. At night her adopters tended to watch television or read and there were rarely other people in the house. Ella had lived in a busy town with streetlights and traffic, but now her home was on the edge of dark countryside. All her sensory environment – sound, light, movement – had changed. Her adopters started leaving lights on around the house and kept the radio on in the kitchen – Ella started to settle as they adjusted her sleep environment and she began to trust that she had not been abandoned, but was just living in a quieter place.

If your child can't settle and cries or wakes in the night, they need reassurance and comfort. Their attachment-seeking behaviour is activated and they need you to meet it. It might go against your own upbringing or what you did with your older birth or other adopted children – when 'controlled crying' and leaving children to cry themselves to sleep were chosen ways of sleep-training. If your child is left to cry, their cortisol levels will rise and stay elevated if they are not soothed – their levels of anxiety and stress will remain high and they will find it very hard to sleep well. They may give up and fall asleep, but given the high level of cortisol still in their system, they may wake often in the night and continue to feel stressed (Sunderland 2006).

Your child may be afraid to let themselves fall asleep or may feel scared that they will go to sleep and wake up to find themselves abandoned. To help them feel safe and to build a secure attachment with you, they need you to help them sleep, rather than being left by themselves to manage their own distress. They need you to soothe them as they are not yet able to do this for themselves. You can choose either to sit with them until they sleep or keep returning to soothe them until they settle. They need a consistent approach so plan this between you if you are a couple and with anyone who is supporting you at bedtime, such as a babysitter.

Some children can take a very long time to learn to settle and it can be an exhausting task. Margot Sunderland has described how this way of teaching them to sleep is best as leaving them to cry is toxic to their brain and to their developing attachment relationships (Sunderland 2006). It will be worth the effort in the long run, but you will need stamina and commitment to do this for your child.

Sometimes your child might wake in the night and call out for you or come and seek you out, standing by your bedside even when you are asleep. You can choose either to take them into your bed or soothe them and return them to their own bed – the key message they need is that they are not alone, that they are safe and you will look after them.

Mealtimes

For children who have experienced neglect, the fear of hunger and worrying about whether they will get fed, such feelings can stay with them even if they have lived with a foster carer who has fed them well. Moving to a new family can trigger anxiety that they or their sibling may go hungry.

> Rosie, aged 12, was found with her four siblings by the police when she was six years old at her birth parent's home. There was no food in the house and all the children were starving. Her adoptive mum and dad described how even after having lived with them for five years, every day when Rosie came home from school the first thing she would do was check the fridge to make sure it had food in it. Shelley always made sure it was well-stocked and they kept a box of snacks next to it, which Rosie could help herself to.

Your child may constantly ask for food even when they have just eaten, or ask about what you'll be having for pudding or tea in the middle of lunch. They may ask for second and third helpings and not seem to know when they are full or they might turn their nose up at what is on their plate and then ask for snacks all day long. They might take food and keep some in their pocket for later, or hide some under their bed just in case. They are trying to ensure that they do not go hungry. They may also feel worried and can mistake this feeling for hunger – eating may be a way for them to help themselves feel better.

When you introduce them to your family routine, place a big emphasis on mealtimes – tell them that each day there will be breakfast, lunch and tea, with snacks in between as well. Feed small children and older ones who have experienced neglect as often as every couple of hours to stabilise their blood sugar levels and teach them that you will meet their need for food. This will help reduce their anxiety and the degree of control they might try to exert over meals and food. Their foster carer will have given you a list of favourite foods and the ones they hate – try to get as much detail as you can about how their food is prepared, so you can offer a similar pattern. Adopters will sometimes say 'she won't eat this, but it says on the list that she loves it' and then feel frustrated that they can't get their child to eat. Remember that in the midst of all the change and in a state of heightened anxiety, your child may be overwhelmed, lose their appetite and try to gain control over what they eat. Check with the foster carer about which brands they use and how they present the food – it might just need some perseverance to help your child feel safe enough to eat the same things at your house.

Mealtimes can become a battle of wills – if your child's survival pattern is to become controlling, then food can become a focus for this. They may refuse to eat or only eat certain things, they may want to eat in front of the television or annoy everyone sitting at the table by eating loudly or kicking under the table so that no one wants to sit next to them. Try to understand how strange it must feel eating at the table with new people in a house they don't know very well. They might be worried they won't like your cooking or what you will do if they don't eat it. If they are squabbling with siblings at the table, they need a higher level of adult supervision to help them manage to eat together –

remember they may not have done this before, or it may remind them of stressful meals in their first home. Encourage them and try to stay calm – avoid a battle of wills that they will win as you can't make them eat.

If you become stressed by your child's refusal to eat, take a break, breathe, get up and refill your water glass and try to regain a sense of empathy for their struggle. Try not to use pudding as a reward, as withholding food can worry them that they may not get enough. Don't worry about how much they eat – most children eat enough to keep themselves going – but check with your health visitor or doctor if you are worried. Rather than introduce lots of new foods, stick with the familiar in the early days.

If they ask you to feed them or cut up their food, even if you think they are old enough to do so themselves, use this as a way to nurture them. They may have missed out on this as a very young child and you can give them this experience of being looked after, as though they had been with you when they were small. Lots of children who have lived in chaotic and neglectful first homes may have eaten limited diets – maybe lots of takeaways, instant snacks, crisps and sweets. They may crave these things, particularly when feeling stressed. They may have eaten at odd times when someone remembered to get food for them, out of packets not from plates, in a pushchair or on the floor. In foster care they may have always eaten with other children, not with adults, or perhaps they ate in a high chair in front of the television – they will have had lots of different mealtime experiences. You may have certain ideas about how you want mealtimes to be in your home, but it helps to balance the introduction of new tastes and ways of eating with remembering their early experiences.

Harry was adopted at age three by Amarjit and Imran – from day one he refused to sit at the table to eat with them. He would grab a piece of food, eat and run from the table. They discovered that his birth mother had been homeless and Harry had spent long periods in his pushchair. When he came into care he had been underweight – his birth mother had given him snacks when she had money and remembered, as she was in a violent and stressful relationship with Harry's father. Once in foster care they had tried to nourish him but he was constantly on the go – his foster carers would follow him around the room and pop a bit of food in his mouth when they could. Amarjit and Imran started again with small snacks. They sat Harry on their laps to feed him, they fed him little and often and talked soothingly to him all the while. Gradually they introduced his 'special' chair at the table – using it at other times to do activities, such as colouring at the table. Harry was reluctant to try anything new: sometimes they managed to get him to eat one pea, then he would refuse any more. But with perseverance and great patience, over time his diet and ability to eat with them improved.

Getting ill

Introductions should come with a health warning! Lots of adopters report catching a cold or feeling unwell during these initial weeks and children often come down with something too. In times of stress, our immune system is suppressed. This makes us more vulnerable to infection (Perry *et al.* 1995; Siegel and Hartzell 2004). Just when you want to feel at your best, you are likely to come down with something. However, this can be an opportunity for bonding. Instead of going out and about, being unwell means you have to slow down and rest. Spending time lying on the sofa, wrapped in soft blankets, with a hot-water bottle and watching films together makes time for relationship-building. Children who are self-reliant and resist being taken care of may let go of this strategy if they are unwell. This will give you an opportunity to nurture them with warm drinks, stroking their head and spending time together, in contrast to what may have happened when they were ill and living with their birth parents.

Billy, aged four, was mid-way through his introductions to Zoe and Cliff when he fell off a climbing-frame and broke his leg. Having lived in a chaotic birth family, Billy was used to taking care of himself. Zoe and Cliff had struggled to make a connection with him during the introductions. After the accident they went with him and the foster carer to the hospital and stayed with him overnight. For the next few weeks, Zoe and Cliff had to carry Billy up and down the stairs, wash and dress him and spend lots of time playing with him, as he couldn't go outside to play. Although they would not advocate this happening to any child, it gave them the opportunity to soothe him when he was in pain and care for him when he was vulnerable. This led to them developing a closer attachment.

School

When older children move to an adoptive family, there is often a debate about when they should start their new school. Some people suggest starting straightaway, as they are already used to the routine of school and benefit from the routine and structure, as well as learning. Others argue that delaying the start of school gives the child a greater opportunity to settle in with their new family. The plans for your child will be made in discussions with their social worker and it may be helpful to consider the decision in the context of their attachment needs.

Although your child may already be attending school or nursery and enjoy going, at this time in their life their primary need is to form a secure and safe attachment relationship with you as their parent. Without this they will struggle to develop – both emotionally and psychologically, and this will impact on their future ability to learn (Bomber 2010). They will struggle to access their thinking brain if they are in a state of high alert and therefore their responses are dictated by their brainstem. This means they will be less able to think, plan and organise themselves, as their priority becomes keeping themselves safe from danger (Siegel and Hartzell 2004). Do not worry that they will miss out on their education, as they will learn well once they have achieved a secure attachment to you. They are not able to learn if they do not feel safe. To feel safe, they need to have developed their attachment relationship with you.

If they are sent to school too early in this phase of their life, it may have a negative impact on their developing relationship with you. The stresses of a new school environment – new teachers, a new peer group, a new building and each new school day could trigger an anxious response in your child. If they are only just starting their relationship with you, they may struggle to manage the demands of school as well. They may resort to survival strategies and the coping mechanisms they have relied on in other stressful situations – such as becoming withdrawn or aggressive with peers (Burnell 2009). Time at home with you before starting school will help them build a secure attachment, so they are better able to meet the challenges of the school day and better able to learn.

Once you decide that your child is ready to start school – and this may not be for a considerable time for some children – meet with the school to plan their transition into school. The school may need some information and training on adoption, attachment and trauma to help them meet the needs of your child – you might ask your social worker to help with this. It will also help the school to understand your child if you can share some of their history – on the agreement that this information be kept confidential and is shared on a need-to-know basis. Some adopters provide a brief description of their child – identifying known triggers and difficulties and outlining strategies to help support them that they have found successful at home. This profile might identify particular times of the day when your child might struggle – such as leaving you at the school gate. A teacher can then understand when they might be vulnerable and provide them during school time with a stable figure who will check with them during the school day to make sure they are feeling all right (Bomber 2010).

Your child might find it hard to believe that you haven't disappeared or that you think about them during the school day

– they have not yet developed that sense of you holding them in your mind – and can feel abandoned. Try putting a little Post-it note in their lunchbox to say that you are thinking about them. You could also make them a key-ring with your photo in it, which they can take with them attached to their pencil case. Encourage them to look at it when they feel sad and are missing you while at school. Giving them a little treasure of yours to keep in their bag to touch when they feel lonely and a spray of your perfume on a hanky to put in their pocket can help them remember your message that you are thinking about them.

Given the demands of the school day, being there at the end of the day to collect them if you can is important. Remember when you have been on a long flight: you come around the corner at arrivals tired, hungry and out of sorts and all you want to see is a familiar face. You might find that your child is grumpy and a bit difficult at the end of the school day – learning to trust that you will be there to meet them and that you will take them home can take time. They may struggle to articulate how hard their day has been and how much they have worried about and missed you.

> Ruby, aged five, started school four weeks after moving to live with Liz and Phil. She had lived in a scary house where both her birth parents had been drug addicts and her birth mother had assaulted Ruby, resulting in her coming into care. If Phil collected her from school, Ruby would rush to be picked up for a cuddle. But if Liz was there, Ruby would run straight past her to another mother and ask to go to her house for tea. Liz was embarrassed by her behaviour, but she stuck it out in the playground – 'I get it,' she told Ruby, 'you don't trust that I can be a good mum to you; but I am going to take care of you and keep you safe.' She explained to some of the other mothers that Ruby was still learning about being in a family and what mothers do – so she was taking her home for tea, maybe she would go to their house another day.

Once home from school, feed your child – don't worry that they won't eat their tea, they most probably will. When they get home they need nurture, regulating and their blood sugar levels need to rebalance – all met by some toast and jam and time on the sofa watching television with you. If you have this time together, the rest of the day will go more smoothly.

Contact with foster carers

Once your child has come to live with you, you will need to consider what contact you will have with their foster carers in the future. You will have been involved in the planning concerning your child's future contact with their birth family (if there is to be any) but sometimes the question of whether they will have contact with their foster carer is not given as much thought. Often at planning meetings a date might be pencilled in but left to be confirmed and it never takes place.

You might have some anxieties about meeting up with the foster carers once your child has moved to join your family. Some adopters worry that their child will be confused by seeing their foster carers again. Other adopters worry that it will unsettle their child when they have only just moved in and they might ask to go home with their foster carer. But it is important not to underestimate the significance of this relationship for your child. Their time spent living with their foster carer might have been their first experience of living in a safe and caring family. If they went to them straight from the hospital they will be the only parents that they have known and if they are an older child they may have formed a particular attachment to them. If they have no further contact, your child may wonder why they don't want to see them or believe that they have disappeared like other people have done in their past. They may feel rejected or abandoned which may inhibit them from forming new attachments with you.

Planning contact will depend on the views of everyone involved but this primarily needs to be led by your child's need to make sense of their move and their story and the relationship they had with the foster carers. The timing of the first visit needs to balance how much progress they have made in settling in and their sense of time – for little children, a month can seem a very long time. The first visit might take place within the first few weeks if everyone feels that they are ready, but for other children they might wait a little longer until they are more settled. Some children, particularly older children, might need a visit sooner as well as telephone contact to help them make the transition. This can feel quite a challenge if you are trying to make a new relationship with a child who is signalling that their previous relationship was so important to them. But acknowledging this allows them to grieve their last relationship while making their new one with you and accepting the change that this brings.

Have the visit at your house and plan it well. Having it at your home signals that this is your child's home now and the foster carers can come and show their approval of where they are living now by admiring their new room and their garden. Talk with your child about who will come, usually just the foster carers and not all their children as the focus needs to be on your child. Plan what you will all do and make sure they are clear that the foster carers will come at a certain time and that they will leave at a certain time – giving the visit a clear structure and a plan will lessen their anxiety about what will happen and give them the message that they are staying with you.

Talk beforehand with the foster carers so you can share any worries you have about what might happen; agree that if your child needs anything, you will help them as you are their parent now. When you are together it gives your child the opportunity to see that all the grown-ups that care about them are positive about what has happened and the move they have made. The foster carers can share that they miss them and are sad they left but they can also give a really strong message that they are happy that they have moved to live with their new family.

This visit can evoke strong emotions for everyone and it can be hard – some foster carers might feel overwhelmed by their loss and feel ambivalent about you taking away the child they have cared for. You might feel guilty about taking away the child they were so close too or worried about upsetting the fragile new attachment you are making with your child. But with support, the visit can be a really positive part of the process. It can help your child with the process of forming their new attachment to you, while accepting the loss of their previous relationship. You might want to consider further contacts as your child grows up so, rather than disappearing from their life, they keep in contact with people who were an important part of it. This might entail visits or keeping in touch with cards – it has to feel right for everyone but is worth considering to show your child that people still think about them and care about them even though they are not living with them anymore (NLAFC 2013).

When things feel difficult

After all the time spent planning and getting ready, you may experience a great sense of elation that you finally have your longed-for family. There will be huge excitement at the first meeting and joy when your child lifts their arms up for a cuddle and calls you mummy or daddy. Your time will suddenly be taken over by hours in the park, building LEGO towers and reading stories – having fun and enjoying doing all the things you imagined doing as a family. However, you may also experience some more difficult emotions and experiences, which you may need some support with. Some adopters describe being bored and a bit deflated – rather than the buzz of excitement they were expecting.

> Brenda and David had just adopted two little boys; when the social worker visited, the boys were happily playing with their cars while their adopters sat watching without joining in. They described feeling quite flat and at a loss as to what they should be doing. They had both taken extended adoption leave from busy, stressful jobs. They had been really looking forward to being at home full-time with the boys so they could devote themselves to building their family life. But they described being 'at home' as quite dull and they felt

bad for not feeling more positive. Acknowledging the huge change they had made and their need to take some time to adjust to their new pace of life enabled them to settle into their new roles as parents.

Other adopters share a sense of feeling under pressure to get things right. They feel watched and judged all the time – by their social workers when they visit, by their own parents and by all the other parents when they take the children out. When your child is first placed, you are in the process of getting to know them and your confidence will grow as you become more familiar with them and with how to look after them.

> Eve described taking Lewis to the supermarket for the first time. He fought being put in the trolley and another shopper came over to help strap him in. He then started screaming as she tried to start the shopping and she gave him some grapes to eat as they went round. At the checkout, he started crying again and she could feel herself getting hotter and hotter as she tried to pack the shopping. She was sure everyone in the queue behind her was thinking what a hopeless mother she was as he got louder and louder. By the time they got to the car she was exhausted and vowed to shop online in future; not a successful first trip.

For some, this sense of being judged leads to a fear of sharing any difficulties they have as they worry they will be deemed to be failing. If they make a mistake, they worry that they might be judged as simply not good enough or that their child will be taken away from them. This can build into a huge sense of pressure to succeed and growing anxiety when things do go wrong. Having this pressure acknowledged by your social worker and your support network can help. It needs naming that this is not like having a birth child – there are people visiting to see how you are doing and they are in a position of power over what happens to your child which can feel very uncomfortable, when you are used to being in control of your life. That underlying fear that they could take your child away can surface when things are difficult. If they can show empathy for this sense of pressure on you to succeed and the fears you may have, you will be better able to share with them the struggles you may be having and also better able to accept support if and when you need it.

Everyone at some point will encounter things they are not sure about or do things they wish they had done differently – being able to share these and learn from your mistakes is the key to making progress when things are challenging. Also, not being too hard on yourself – particularly if you have a tendency to try to be perfect – is important. Joining a group of other adopters who are going through the same experiences can be really helpful. Once you hear how many other people have lost their temper trying to get everyone ready for school in the morning or have separated squabbling siblings with threats that they will never play with that toy again, you may not judge yourself so harshly. You may feel under huge pressure as an adoptive parent to get it right – but everyone makes mistakes and no one gets it right all of the time. The critical thing to remember is to repair any rupture in your relationship with your child – and there will always be more opportunities to make a connection with them (Hughes and Baylin 2012).

Other adopters express a sense of disappointment with the adoption process – somehow it was not what they were expecting and they need time to explore and understand these feelings. They describe the intensity of expectations in introductions as feeling overwhelming – being called mummy for the first time by a child they do not know makes them feel pressured to love them when they do not know how they feel. They may struggle to feel what they think they ought to feel towards their child and somehow feel much sadder and more ambivalent. They may experience a sense of mourning for what they have missed or what might have been – not being there when this child first smiled or when they needed keeping safe. Previous losses, the experience of infertility and unresolved issues from their past can lead some adopters to feeling sad and depressed. You may find yourself experiencing similar emotions and may need support from your partner, family and social worker to help you with these feelings and resolve any issues that may be triggered by the adoption process. It can be really hard to acknowledge that you are having these feelings, but if you can share them you can receive the support that you need.

Sometimes adopters experience a sudden, acute emotional crisis and have been unable to carry on with introductions or with the adoption. They have not been able to engage with their child, have started to spend less time with them or have found ways to be absent – going out, going to work, spending time in another room away from their child or not getting out of bed. They have become tearful and withdrawn or go through the motions of caring for their child without emotionally engaging with them. They may have become irritable or angry with everyone without just cause. This can shock and puzzle those around them as they struggle to understand how they can reject something they have been wanting for so long. They may have made all the right preparations, decorated their room, bought them lovely clothes and stopped work. Their child may be the right age, present no problems or challenges and may be seeking them out as their mummy or daddy – but still they feel they cannot be this child's parent and may decide not to continue.

There are a myriad of factors that can lead to this acute emotional crisis for adopters – the match may not be right, they may have unresolved losses that overwhelm them or the arrival of this child may have activated their trigger points regarding issues from their own attachment history.

In their book *Brain-Based Parenting* (Hughes and Baylin 2012), Dan Hughes and John Baylin describe how being under extreme stress can disrupt an adult's ability to care, give nurture and have empathy for other people. Their model explains how the brain is affected by stress and how this impacts on the parent's care-giving system, impeding care-giving and giving rise to 'blocked care'. In introductions and the early days of adoption, parents will be under extreme stress and there may well be triggers that give rise to blocked care – both acute and child-specific. It will be acute given the intense nature of introductions and the early weeks of creating a new relationship. It may be also be child-specific. Hughes and Baylin identify how a particular child can trigger a trauma response in the adult. The adult is then no longer able to care for the child and this results in a state of blocked care. There may be something about the way the child looks or behaves that triggers them into a response linked to their own history, for example, the way their own parent looked after them. Or the child may not respond positively to the care given, pushing them away or preferring the other parent; this can also start to shut down their care-giving. If this happens, adopters need support to discover what has triggered this acute response in themselves and discover whether they can reactivate their emotional ability to care for this child. Although during the matching process this child may have seemed the perfect one for these adopters, there may be something about the interaction between them that is played out only once they are actually in each others' physical presence that causes this to occur.

Adopters are encouraged at every step to share any worries or concerns they may have but sometimes it may have been too difficult to even name what they are feeling, given the possible consequences of sharing such fears and doubts. Sometimes it is only with the benefit of looking back that the reasons why things became so difficult start to appear. Using this way of thinking about what is happening can help both professionals and adopters involved in such difficult situations begin to understand what was happening and plan a way forward. When introductions are disruptive and the adoption does not go ahead, everyone involved needs support – the person who has given up their chance to parent, their partner who may not have felt the same about this child, and their other children who were expecting to have a brother or sister. They will need reassurance that the child who was going to live with them will be safe and looked after by their foster carer; they will also need time to grieve their loss. Professionals need to acknowledge that they may also feel intense emotions about what has happened and ensure that these do not spill over into their relationship with the adopters. Children who have been prepared for an adoption which does not go ahead need support to make sense of what has happened as part of their life-story, rather than anyone rushing to look for another family for them.

As you read this, you may think that this won't happen to you – but if you are struggling with your feelings about your child, using this way of thinking to help you understand what is going on and sharing this with people close to you can help you plan a way forward.

CHAPTER NINE

● ● ● ● ● ● ● ● ● ●

Conclusion

As an adopter you want to create a happy and safe family life with your child. However, your child may have experienced very difficult early life experiences which will have had a profound impact on them. The challenge is how to shape your family to enable your child to feel secure in your family and to heal from the effects of their early experiences. The idea for writing this book came from thinking about how best to begin this process. If the process of introductions is informed by ideas from research on attachment, trauma and loss then it will be better shaped to meet your needs as an adoptive family. In this way the process would take account of your child's early experiences and their need for attachment-based parenting to help them settle and thrive in your family.

My hope is that using this framework of attachment and trauma to inform the planning meetings, the preparations that you make and how your child is prepared to say goodbye to their foster carers and helped to understand why they are moving will enable everyone to be best placed for the next part of the process. That using this framework will shape the first meetings and the actual move in a way that helps everyone to acknowledge the emotional intensity of the process and the need to support everyone involved and give the process enough time. And finally, that the ideas for creating family routines and dealing with some of the challenges you may face will help you achieve the happy and secure family life you set out to create from the very beginning.

I hope that the social workers and family who are supporting you in this process will also find these ideas helpful so they can understand what you need and how best to support you as you begin your life as an adoptive family.

Bibliography

Archer, K. (2012) *First Steps in Parenting the Child Who Hurts*. London: Jessica Kingsley Publishers.

Argent, H. (2010) *Adopting a Brother or Sister*. London: BAAF.

Argent, H. (2011) *Related by Adoption: Handbook for Grandparents and Other Relatives*. London: BAAF.

Argent, H. (2012) *Moving Pictures*. London: BAAF.

Ayres, J. (1991) *A Parent's Guide to Understanding Sensory Integration*. Torrance, CA: S.I. International.

Bhreathnach, E. (2009) 'Trauma, sensory processing and attachment. Sensory-attachment intervention.' Conference paper presented at the Family Futures Conference, London, UK. Available at www.sensoryattachmentintervention.com/Documents/Trauma%20FFrCwv.doc, accessed on 29 May 2014.

Bomber, L. (2007) *Inside I'm Hurting*. London: Worth Publishing.

Bomber, L. (2010) *What about Me?* London: Worth Publishing.

Bowlby, J. (1973) *Attachment and Loss, Volume II, Separation: Anxiety and Anger*. New York, NY: Basic Books.

Bowlby, J. (1980) *Attachment and Loss, Volume III, Loss: Sadness and Depression*. New York, NY: Basic Books.

Bowlby, J. (1982) *Attachment and Loss, Volume I, Attachment (second edition)*. New York, NY: Basic Books.

Bowlby, J. (1998) *A Secure Base: Clinical Applications of Attachment Theory*. London: Routledge.

Brown, R. and Ward, H. (2013) 'Decision-making within a child's time-frame: An overview of current research evidence for family justice professionals concerning child development and the impact of maltreatment.' Working Paper 16 (2nd ed.). London: Childhood Wellbeing Research Centre. Available at www.gov.uk/government/uploads/system/uploads/attachment_data/file/200471/Decision-making_within_a_child_s_timeframe.pdf, accessed on 29 May 2014.

Brudnage, K. and Gentry, D. (2005) *Reducing Separation Trauma: A Manual for Foster Parents, Social Workers and Community Members who Care for Children and Youth.* State University of New York, NY. Counselling School and Educational Psychology.

Burnell, A. (2009) 'Planning transitions for children moving to permanent placement: What do you do after you say "hello"?' *Family Futures Practice Paper Series.* London: Family Futures. Available at www.familyfutures.co.uk/wp-content/uploads/2012/11/Transitions-Practice-Paper.pdf, accessed on 9 September 2014.

Byrne, S. (2000) *Linking and Introductions Guidelines.* London: BAAF.

Cohen, L. (2001) *Playful Parenting.* New York: Ballantine Books, Random House Publishing.

Dozier, M. (2003) 'Attachment-based treatment for vulnerable children.' *Attachment and Human Development 5*, 3, 253–257.

Fahlberg, V. (2012) *A Child's Journey through Placement.* London: BAAF.

Foxon, J. (2001) *Nutmeg Gets Adopted.* London: BAAF.

Gerhardt, S. (2004) *Why Love Matters.* Hove: Routledge.

Golding, K. (2008) *Nurturing Attachments: Supporting Children Who Are Fostered or Adopted.* London: Jessica Kingsley Publishers.

Golding, K. and Hughes, D. (2012) *Creating Loving Attachments.* London: Jessica Kingsley Publishers.

Gray, D. (2012a) *Attaching in Adoption: Practical Tools for Today's Parents.* London: Jessica Kingsley Publishers.

Gray, D. (2012b) *Nurturing Adoptions.* London: Jessica Kingsley Publishers.

Howe, D. (2005) *Child Abuse and Neglect: Assessment, Development and Intervention.* Basingstoke: Palgrave MacMillan.

Hughes, D. (2006) *Building the Bonds of Attachment: Awakening Love in Deeply Troubled Children.* Lanham, MD: Jason Aronson.

Hughes, D. (2009) *Attachment-Focused Parenting: Effective Strategies to Care for Children.* New York, NY: Norton.

Hughes, D. (2013, November) 'The place for parenting'. Paper presented at the Adoption UK Conference, Birmingham, UK. Available at www.adoptionuk.org/sites/default/files/documents/HTAGM%202013%20speech.pdf, accessed on 29 May 2014.

Hughes, D. and Baylin, J. (2012) *Brain-Based Parenting: The Neuroscience of Caregiving for Healthy Attachment.* New York, NY: Norton.

Jernberg, A.M. and Booth, P.B. (2010). *Theraplay: Helping Parents and Children Build Better Relationships Through Attachment-based Play.* San Fransisco, CA: Wiley and Sons.

Kaniuk, J., Steele, M. and Hodges, J. (2004) 'Report on a longitudinal research project, exploring the development of attachments between older, hard-to-place children and their adopters over the first two years of placement.' *Adoption and Fostering 28*, 2, 61–67.

Koomar, J. (2009) 'Trauma and attachment-informed sensory integration assessment.' *Sensory Integration 32*, 4. Available at http://attachmentcoalition.org/yahoo_site_admin/assets/docs/SIandAtt.4101942.pdf, accessed on 29 May 2014.

Kübler-Ross, E. (1969) *On Death and Dying.* New York: Macmillan.

Laurie, C. (2013) 'I'm on the sensory diet.' *Your Autism 47*, 4, 37–39.

Macliver, C. and Thom, M. (1990) *Family Talk*. London: BAAF.

Moran, H. (2010) 'Introductions and the early days of placement.' Unpublished paper. Coventry: Trauma, Attachment and Preparation for Placement Training Course, Coventry Social Services.

North London Adoption and Fostering Consortium (NLAFC) (2013) *Adoption Support Handbook*. London: NLAFC. Available at www.camden.gov.uk/theme/cl../ccm/cms-service/download/asset/?asset_id=3185672, accessed on 30 May 2014.

Norris, V. and Twigger, S. (2013) *Supporting Transition to a New Family – An Attachment and Trauma-Based Approach*. Hereford: The Family Place. Available at www.thefamilyplace.co.uk, accessed on 30 May 2014.

National Scientific Council on the Developing Child (NSCDC) (2004) *Children's Emotional Development is Built in the Architecture of their Brains: Working Paper 2*. Boston, MA: Center on the Developing Child, Harvard University. Available at http://developingchild.harvard.edu/resources/reports_and_working_papers/working_papers/wp2, accessed on May 30 2014.

NSCDC (2009) *Excessive Stress Disrupts the Architecture of the Developing Brain: Working Paper 3*. Boston, MA: Center on the Developing Child, Harvard University. Available at http://developingchild.harvard.edu/index.php/resources/reports_and_working_papers/working_papers/wp3, accessed on May 30 2014.

Perry, B. (2001) *Bonding and Attachment in Maltreated Children: Consequences of Emotional Neglect in Childhood*. Houston, TX: ChildTrauma Academy. Available at www.cpri.ca/uploads/section000181/files/bonding%20and%20attachment%20in%20maltreated%20children.pdf, accessed on May 30 2014.

Perry, B. (2002) 'Childhood experience and the expression of genetic potential: What childhood neglect tells us about nature and nurture.' *Brain and Mind 3*, 79–100.

Perry, B. (2006) 'Applying principles of neurodevelopment to clinical work with maltreated children: A neurosequential model of therapeutics.' In N. Webb (ed.) *Working with Traumatized Youth in Child Welfare*. New York, NY: Guildford Press.

Perry, B. (2009) 'Examining child maltreatment through a neurodevelopmental lens: Clinical Applications of the neurosequential model of therapeutics'. *Journal of Loss and Trauma 14*, 240–255.

Perry, B. (2010) *Introduction to the Neurosequential Model of Therapeutics*. Houston, TX: ChildTrauma Academy. Available at www.eusarf2012.org/Portals/13/Documents/nmt_core_slides_2011.pdf, accessed 30 May 2014.

Perry, B. and Pollard, D. (1997) 'Altered brain development following global neglect in early childhood.' *Society for Neuroscience: Proceedings from Annual Meeting*, New Orleans.

Perry, B. and Szlalvitz, M. (2006) *The Boy Who Was Raised as a Dog*. New York, NY: Basic Books.

Perry, B., Pollard, R., Blakely, T., Baker, W. and Vigilante, D. (1995) 'Childhood trauma, the neurobiology of adaptation and use-dependent development of the brain: How states become traits.' *Infant Mental Health Journal 16*, 4, 271–291.

Radwan, K. (2009) 'Sensory attachment integration.' *Adoption Today October 2009*, 20–21.

Rees, J. (2009) *Life-Story Books for Adopted Children: A Family Friendly Approach*. London: Jessica Kingsley Publishers.

Ryan, T. and Walker, R. (2007) *Life-Story Work: A Practical Guide to Help Children Understand Their Past*. London: BAAF.

Saunders, H., Selwyn, J. and Fursland, E. (2013) *Placing Large Sibling Groups for Adoption*. London: BAAF.

Schofield, G., and Beck, M. (2006) *Attachment Handbook for Fosters Care and Adoption*. London: BAAF.

Scully, T. (2013) 'Regulating the traumatised child and their parents through the use of sensory attachment and body-based techniques.' Paper presented at British Association of Play Therapists conference, June 2013, Birmingham, UK.

Siegel, D. and Hartzell, M. (2004) *Parenting from the Inside Out*. New York, NY: Penguin.

Sprince, J. (2013) 'Thinking towards belonging.' *Seen and Heard 23*, 2, 34–45.

Stubbs, D., Sokes, J., Alilovic and Baker, H. (2009) *A Child's Grief: Supporting a Child When Someone in their Family has Died*. Cheltenham: Winston's Wish.

Sunderland, M. (2006) *The Science of Parenting*. New York, NY: Dorling Kindersley.

Van der Kolk, B. (1994) 'The body keeps the score: Memory and the evolving psychobiology of post-traumatic stress.' *Harvard Review of Psychiatry 1*, 5, 253–265.

Van der Kolk, B. (2005) 'Developmental trauma disorder: Towards a rational diagnosis for children with complex trauma histories.' *Psychiatric Annals 35*, 5, 401–408.

Verrier, N. (1993) *The Primal Wound: Understanding the Adopted Child*. Baltimore, MD: Gateway Press.

Walsh, M., Rose, R. and Philpot, T. (2004) *The Child's Own Story: Life-Story Work with Traumatized Children*. London: Jessica Kingsley Publishers.

Books for Children

Alper, J. (2002) *Billy Says* series. Newport Pagnell: Fosterplus.

Alper, J. (2008) *All About Mummies and Daddies*. Bedfordshire: Adoptionplus.

Argent, H. (2007) *Josh and Jaz Have Three Mums*. London: BAAF.

Argent, H. (2010) *Adopting a Brother or Sister*. London: BAAF.

Bagnell, S. (2008) *The Teazles' Baby Bunny*. London: BAAF.

Betts, B. and Ball, N. (2004) *Bridget's Taking a Long Time*. Information Plus. Available via BAAF catalogue.

Bhreathnach, E. (2012) *The Scared Gang*. Ballynahinch, Northern Ireland: Alder Tree Press.

Brodzinsky Braff, A. (2014) *Can I Tell You about Adoption?* Buckingham: Hinton House.

Bruzzone, C. and Morton, L. (2013) *All About Me*. London: B Small Publishing.

Cole, B. (1995) *Mummy Laid an Egg!* London: Red Fox Picture Books.

Daniels, R. (2009) *Finding a Family for Tommy*. London: BAAF.

Edwards, B. (2010) *The Most Precious Present in the World*. London: BAAF.

Foxon, J. (2001) *Nutmeg Gets Adopted* series. London: BAAF.

Friday, C. (2005) *Oh, Brother!* Totten: Adoption UK.

Gliori, D. (1999) *No Matter What*. London: Bloomsbury.

Ironside, V. (1996) *The Huge Bag of Worries*. London: Hodder.

Kahn, H. (2002) *Tia's Wishes/Tyler's Wishes*. London: BAAF.

Levinson, Gilman, J. (2009) *Murphy's Three Homes*. Washington, DC: Magination Press.

Lidster, A. (2012) *Chester and Daisy Move On*. London: BAAF.

Merchant, E. (2010) *Dad David, Baba Chris and Me*. London: BAAF.

Meredith, E. (2001) *Where Do Babies Come From?* London: Usborne.

Nemiroff, M. and Annuziata, J. (2004) *All About Adoption*. Washington, DC: Maginaton Press.

Ross, T. (2005) *I Don't Want to Go to Sleep*. London: Harper Collins Books.

Sambrooks, P. (2009) *Denis the Duckling.* London: BAAF.

Sambrooks, P. (2011) *Denis and the Big Decisions.* London: BAAF.

Sunderland, M. (2000) *A Nifflenoo Called Nevermind.* Oxon: Winslow Press.

Sunderland, M. (2003) *How Hattie Hated Kindness.* Bicester: Speechmark.

Sunderland, M. (2003) *The Day the Sea Went Out and Never Came Back.* Bicester: Speechmark.

Thomas, P. (2003) *My New Family: A First Look at Adoption.* New York: Barrons Educational Series.

Voake, C. (2003) *Ginger Finds a New Home.* London: Walker.

Index

11935564R00116

Made in the USA
Lexington, KY
17 October 2018